Whole Happy and Healthy
A Revolutionary Approach to Understanding and Thriving with Mental Illness

Jessica R. Dreistadt

Whole Happy and Healthy: A Revolutionary Approach to Understanding and Thriving with Mental Illness

ISBN 978-1543273380

The information presented in this book represents the informed opinion of the author and is not intended to diagnose or treat a medical condition. This book and its contents should not be relied upon as a sole source of information related to mental illness. This book represents a complementary resource to help readers help themselves. If you are in need of assistance due to mental illness or any other condition, please consult professional practitioners as needed.

The Fruition Coalition
Lehigh Valley, PA
www.fruitioncoalition.com
www.jessicardreistadt.com

Table of Contents

Chapter One
The Experience of Mental Illness

I have never dared to take my life for granted. Doing so would be impossible, because I have worked very hard to remain alive every day for nearly thirty years. As one of more than 450 million people around the world (according to the World Health Organization) who is currently experiencing the challenge of mental illness, my life is at once perilous and precious. It is perilous because it is wrought with agonizing, debilitating emotional pain. It is precious because my heart's capacity for patience, compassion, understanding, forgiveness, and love has been expanded through these continual, and cumulative, difficulties.

I was born special, as we all are. My particular specialness was a peculiarity that has been labeled in many ways throughout my life, most recently as bipolar disorder with obsessive compulsive, borderline, and paranoid features. At 14, I was placed in a mental institution where I was diagnosed with schizotypal personality disorder. After that came post-traumatic stress disorder. Major depressive disorder. Generalized anxiety disorder. Disorder, disorder, disorder.

Through this disorder, this chaos, great beauty and wisdom have emerged. Whenever my heart is torn apart, it is left more open and tender. Each moment of angst has led to greater clarity of my purpose and priorities. Every emotional breakdown has resulted in a stronger and more persistent sense of inner peace. My life challenges have been opportunities for me to become more self-aware, learn, transform, and flourish. My mental illness must be my gift to the world because it has filled my life with a richness and beauty that I otherwise would not have been able to experience — and because I cannot conscionably allow it to contribute toward destruction and devastation.

Mental illness, both the diagnostic labels that have been assigned to me and my everyday thoughts and emotions, has defined and confined much of my life. I cannot exist separately from my mental illness; it is intrinsically integrated into everything I think, feel, and do. It isn't something I can set aside when it becomes an inconvenience; it is always with me. The pervasive nature of my mental illness has been exacerbated by the diagnoses I have been given throughout my life. Not only does my mental illness impose real limits on my ability to think and feel with clarity, my diagnoses only seem to affirm that I am in some way deficient and unable to fully function. The way I understand myself, both through my own experience and others' interpretation of my behavior, has become distorted and limited by the mystique of mental illness.

All of my social encounters, both personal and professional, are tainted by acute feelings of difference. I feel as though this shadow of difference follows me wherever I go and partially obscures what lies within me and before me. I never enter a relationship, or even a conversation, from a place of 'normal;' rather, I begin each encounter feeling somewhat defensive and depleted. I feel that others can sense my difference, and that they will inevitably find that I somehow fall short of their expectations. Moments spent in the company of others can be exhausting because I am waiting for them to discover all of the many things that are supposedly wrong with me and working hard to ensure that this doesn't happen in a traumatizing and embarrassing way.

Being a person who has been diagnosed with bipolar disorder means that there are nights when I am wide awake and days when I have to force myself to get out of bed. It is to live with continual intrigue, excitement, and imminent danger. It is to be a living paradox. It is a life of silent unpredictability, instability, insatiability, and impending chaos that can simultaneously be terrifying and exhilarating.

Despite the challenges of living with a mental illness, I am doing fairly well by many measures. I have two master's degrees and have made significant progress toward a doctorate. I have written and published 10 books. I am a homeowner. I had a somewhat prolific job, at least by local standards, with a great deal of responsibility by the time I was 30 years old and maintained that job for six years, leaving voluntarily to pursue other opportunities. I am respected in my professional field. I have colleagues, friends, and relatives that I trust and adore. I do my laundry every week, balance my checkbook, and eat regular, healthy meals — at least most of the time! I feel fulfilled and in love with my life even though my life, from the inside out, is very different from what is commonly accepted as 'normal' and despite the fact that there are moments when I still experience deep emotional pain.

Getting to this place where I feel as though I am somewhat successful, not only by external measures but internally as well, and where I can feel appreciative of the lessons my mental illness has taught me, has been a long and difficult road to navigate. In my young life, I experienced years of darkness and desperation in which I was barely able to function. I thought and did things of which I am truly ashamed. I did poorly in school, reflected by bad grades and turbulent social interactions, I felt alone and misunderstood, I was haunted by insecurity and rage, and I had little real hope for the future. I submerged into a world mostly of my own making to cope with my inner turmoil as well as the harsh world that failed to accept me for who I was.

More recently, I have continued to struggle to fully feel that my life was peaceful and vibrant despite a more confident and successful outward appearance. Some of my diary entries reveal evidence of this duality:

- my life feels out of control in every area;
- just now I feel so dead, dry, depressed;
- I have felt overwhelmingly helpless for the past few months;
- today I feel tired and my thoughts are racing. I barely slept for two nights;
- feeling lost, alone, hopeless, distrustful, worried, sad;
- my life feels so stagnant. I'm trapped and I'm going to violently burst out one day;
- I am unsure of who I am and what I really want to do with my life; and
- I feel dead, lonely, and empty. Disgusting. Non-human, I feel ashamed of myself. I am afraid that no one will ever love me.

Although by the time I wrote these passages I had started to find my way in life, with a stronger identity, meaningful vocation, and loving relationships in place, I was not able to fully release my tumultuous past. I had become accustomed to not feeling emotionally well, which had become my 'normal.'

Those dark, scary places in my heart have been slowly and delicately illuminated through a meticulous but joyous process of self-exploration and acceptance. I found a bright light within and submerged myself in its warm, healing rays. I discovered springtime in my soul, a process for replenishment and rejuvenation when life feels stark and cold. This illumination continues with cumulative effects, revealing to me more and more beautiful aspects of myself and of the world in which I live. While I still have moments, and even weeks, when I fall back into those harsh, frenzied spaces, my experiences of healing stay within me and pull me through even the most difficult of times.

I have decided to share my story through this book for several reasons. Throughout the past 30 or so years, I have experienced a variety of traditional mental health treatments, most of which have not truly helped me, under the care of several well-meaning medical professionals. Many of the treatments that I received were in fact harmful. My prescription medications have caused me to pass out while taking a shower and to fall down half of a flight of stairs. I have felt judged, misunderstood, humiliated, and even abused after engaging in sessions of talk therapy. It is experiences such as these that can result in the unintended consequence of people who experience mental illness simultaneously feeling more desperate and more resistant to seeking help.

Like the medical industry which treats disease, my mental health treatment has primarily been focused on the acute presenting symptoms rather than the natural means by which my thoughts, emotions, and senses are capable of working together toward a more whole and fulfilled self. Traditional mental health treatment is, in my experience, designed to demonize and minimize the few, albeit often gravely serious things that are deemed to be 'wrong' rather than develop and propagate the many things that are 'right.' It is about tipping the scales against a supposed internal enemy rather than discovering and balancing the love and hate, good and bad, and wrong and right that exists inside us all to promote productivity and vitality. I am not suggesting that mainstream mental health treatment is not useful or even critically important, but that a holistic approach that integrates alternative modalities and leverages the efficacy of the person suffering from mental illness would have been more effective for me. And I believe that this approach would also be effective for many, though not necessarily all, others.

While mental illness is perceived to be an internal adversary, people who are experiencing mental illness are too often either demonized or glorified — or both — in our society. People who are mentally ill are frequently perceived to be scary and dangerous. Conversely, we are often seen as extraordinary and fascinating. Reactions to people who are experiencing mental illness range from horror to intrigue to pity to apathy. All of these reactions are normal and are not necessarily unkind; however, it is a great disservice to emphasize abnormality rather than humanity. Through this book, I hope to challenge the prevailing views about people with a mental health diagnosis and to move us all closer to sincere curiosity, understanding, acceptance, and appreciation.

As a person who has experienced mental illness ranging from a mild nuisance to a disabling burden throughout most of my life, I am a native expert in the field. By sharing the laboratory of my life, dissecting my personal experiences, and analyzing my thoughts and feelings under a microscope, I hope to discover and share intellectual, emotional, and behavioral processes that contribute to a more emotionally balanced life. I find myself uniquely positioned to offer to you and to the world new ways of understanding mental illness that will change the way we prevent emotional blocks, remove barriers, and promote healing.

I want this book to be useful and to make a real difference for people who suffer from emotional distress and mental illness as well as those who love and care for them. I endeavor to empower and inspire all of us through the creative generation of practical and impactful ideas. My highest aspiration is to help people who are suffering find peace through guided self-discovery that uncovers previously unrealized opportunities for understanding and transformation.

As a person who is insatiably inquisitive, I am compelled to explore alternatives to mainstream mental health diagnosis and treatment. We cannot be satisfied that we have reached the pinnacle of mental health treatment when there are so many millions of people all around the world who are agonizing and even dying because of mental illness. My conscience and my curiosity combine to energize this search for new and unique solutions.

Through this journey, I hope to demystify both mental illness and some of the alternative approaches that can be used to not just effectively manage these dis-eases, but to heal and to thrive. In this book, I will explore the wilderness of my heart so that together we can discover new ways of understanding mental and emotional differences as well as innovative means to use those differences to our advantage.

Mental illness can be overwhelming, even debilitating. My approach to living well with mental illness has been based on small, simple, sustainable life choices. These modest but significant steps have made a profound difference in my daily life. By sharing these concepts with you, we can all benefit and grow.

Finally, writing this book is a significant part of my own healing journey. As I encounter middle age, I am at a point in my life where things are starting to 'click.' I have developed the ability to recognize and more clearly comprehend the mistakes I have made in the past so that I can better prioritize how I use my precious time left on earth into the future. I am filled with many more questions than answers, but those questions are pointing me toward deeper and more meaningful ways of understanding my life's purpose and direction as well as the meaning that mental illness has had in my life.

I have a strong desire to help the world heal. My own illumination is burning a fire within my heart that yearns to spread so that many more hearts can be illuminated. Helping others learn and heal is a huge part of my life purpose, so the very act of writing this book is making me feel more centered and happy in my life. Additionally, I am continually seeking my special something that will make our world a better place. Like most people, I yearn to make a mark, to matter. I hope that my unique experience and perspective on this topic changes the realm of possibilities for people who suffer with or because of mental illness; this is my one of my most significant gifts to the world.

Living with mental illness means living with many daily difficulties. As we begin this journey together, I am going to uncover and describe some of those challenges that often lie beyond our immediate field of understanding. Because having a mental illness is both a personal and a social challenge, I will explore this phenomenon from both perspectives.

People who experience mental illness often also struggle with low self-esteem. For me, my self-esteem is always on a roller coaster; it can be sky high one moment and below sea level the next. As a person who experiences such ups and downs, low self-esteem feels particularly low in contrast to its intermittent highs. Closely tied to self-esteem is my self-concept and self-perception. The way I perceive myself — my strengths, challenges, dreams, work, and responses to interactions with others — impact how I feel about and value myself. When I make a mistake, my self-esteem plummets. When I complete an important and complicated project, it soars. My self-worth is too often tied to my external actions and interactions rather than an intrinsic, consistent feeling of value as a human being. I may be partially hardwired this way, but the label of mental illness has also negatively impacted my self-esteem. Being classified with diagnoses such as 'bipolar' and 'schizotypal' have on some level caused me to feel that who I am is not enough and needs to be changed to meet a standard that is honestly impossible, and even undesirable, for me to achieve.

Routine daily self-care can also be a challenge. I sometimes get so lost in my head that I neglect the rest of my body. Sleep, which is vital to all aspects of physical and emotional health, is too often interrupted by bouts of insomnia or obsessive worry that makes it difficult to drift off into a soft slumber. I love to exercise, but sometimes get into ruts where it is difficult to prioritize my time and work it into my schedule. I never have a problem with daily showering or bathing, because I am a control freak who is perhaps neurotically grossed out when I miss a day, or by any kind of germs or contamination for that matter. For some people, these and other self-care routines might require energy and attention that are not available. Brushing your teeth might seem like an exercise in futility when the world appears to be crashing in all around you.

Other daily routines can also be a challenge. For some people, it can be difficult to establish daily work, meal preparation, household chore, and other routines that make life flow more easily. Others, like me, keep a fairly rigid schedule that is packed tight with productive projects and tasks. In my case, my routines run my life. Despite this contrived consistency, I can be thrillingly spontaneous and gravely disappointed when others do not share my immediate sense of adventure.

Another ongoing challenge for me and for others who experience mental illness is suppression of the self. Because we are told that we are not good enough as we are and that we need to change for our own good, we can sometimes push back our true selves to appear 'normal' and to make it easier to function in an unaccepting world. We suppress ourselves in many ways, including our thoughts, our feelings, our words, our behavior, how we dress and present ourselves, and how we interact with other people. There are times when temporary suppression is necessary, particularly when we are at risk of becoming a danger to ourselves or to others. But too often we suppress and repress other parts of ourselves to fit in rather than letting our uniqueness shine forth. This self-denial negatively impacts self-esteem and makes it impossible to truly heal and flourish.

We also cut ourselves off from the world through isolation. Isolation can be either physical or emotional. Through physical isolation, we intentionally remove ourselves from potentially painful social interactions that might jeopardize our internal sense of security and serenity. Through emotional isolation, we distance ourselves from others in a number of ways. We often need to keep our mental health diagnosis under wraps to prevent being judged or misunderstood. In the workplace, it would be awkward and probably deemed unprofessional to talk about our personal challenges in a meaningful way. We may hide our diagnosis from new friends to preserve the relationship. I have had a few experiences in my life where I shared my diagnosis and then was quickly abandoned and excluded from a social group. It is easier to not share information about my mental illness, even though it is the only constant in my life, so that I do not risk losing companionship. We can also keep our mental illness a secret by camouflaging our behavior so that no one suspects that we are different in this way. Doing this has led me to feel a tremendous amount of shame and guilt and at times to even feel like a fraud. These feelings compound those that derive from my unique mental and emotional composition.

Relationships can be difficult for people who are experiencing mental illness. Starting a new relationship or deepening one that already exists can be terrifying, provoking anxiety and emotional imbalance. Other people can be triggers for our internal challenges. I can sometimes be doing well emotionally when I am, through an interaction with an innocent unknowing person, suddenly devastated by repeated thoughts about how that other person misunderstands or has hurt me. At the same time, I often misinterpret other people's intentions. In these cases, I am projecting my own fears and insecurities about myself onto others and expecting the worst. I also struggle with jealousy. I am not so sinister as to have experienced Schadenfreude, the feeling of pleasure that derives from other people's misfortune, but I am not always appreciative of the success experienced by others when my life feels wrought with setbacks. I say not always, because I do sincerely care about other people and on the deepest level I want all people in the world to experience joy and happiness. I just sometimes forget that in those moments when I am feeling frustrated and blocked in my own life.

Managing finances can be another area of challenge for many people who experience mental illness. I can be impulsive and even reckless; my finances have unfortunately not been immune to this behavior. As most of us have done from time to time, I have purchased things that I didn't really need only to find later that those things took up too much space in my home and sapped a lot of my energy. My financial choices have also been influenced by the way I value, or devalue, myself. When I feel as though my personal self-worth is deficient, I sometimes compound the issue by destroying my financial worth as well through unnecessary spending to fulfill that perceived need. My spending and savings habits have also been influenced by a distortion of my time orientation. When I am not fully immersed in the present moment, I may purchase things that heal old wounds or fail to save because I think there will be plenty of time to do that in the future in which I will surely be more financially secure than I am now.

Completing tasks and projects has been another challenge in my life. My head is always spinning with millions of ideas and the volume of possibilities can be overwhelming. I am sometimes able to latch onto an idea and bring it out into the world through some type of project. While I have seen many projects through to completion in my life, there are many more that remain in various stages of progress. Not only am I pulled in too many directions, but my neurotic perfectionism also makes it difficult for me to finish projects. I want things to be done well, to my impossibly high standards. Starting a project is somewhat like giving birth; an idea is conceived and brought to life with a lot of love, patience, and nurturing. Finishing a project is like having a child leave the nest; it can be hard to let go and to move on.

These are just some of the personal challenges that I have experienced in relation to mental illness. There are many more, and every person has their own unique challenges related to living with mental illness. The ways we interpret those experiences are influenced by our personality, values, priorities, and upbringing, but our understanding is also influenced by many social and cultural factors.

I live in the United States. In the Western world, we live in a culture of dichotomies and there is a lot of artificial division in our society. Things and people are understood in contrast with their opposite. For example, what it means to be poor is often explored through comparisons with people who are wealthy. What it means to be a woman can be (but shouldn't be) described in comparison to the generalized characteristics of men. This comparative and competitive culture leads to great dis-ease. Seeing the world in black and white rather than as a limitless field of vibrant possibilities robs life of its sacred beauty and mystery. When we understand ourselves, even in part, in contrast to a 'standard,' we fail to appreciate ourselves as unique living expressions of love. People who experience mental illness are not only labeled and judged, we are categorized as inferior to the standards of sanity and normality. The ability to perceive that people who experience mental illness are both unique and share hopes and dreams for their lives that are similar to others' can sometimes be lost.

Difference can arouse suspicion, particularly when its manifestations are unknown. Any type of difference can trigger an emotional reaction of which we are often unaware. It is a subtle form of prejudice, because it is unnoticed and therefore unnamed and accepted as normal. People who experience mental illness are subject to a great deal of judgment; we can be perceived as detached, unkind, or even dangerous if nothing but our diagnosis is known. We are sometimes ignored and excluded so that others can feel safe. It is fully acceptable, even rewarded, in our culture to socially segregate on the basis of mental and emotional difference.

People who experience mental illness are directly or indirectly understood as fragmented and incomplete. My bipolar diagnosis implies that within me there are two competing characteristics: depression and mania. These pathological aspects of my temperament are often described as distinct and disconnected rather than complementary parts of a greater whole. As a person with a mental health diagnosis, I can also be considered incomplete; who I am, as I am, is not adequate in comparison to the normal standard. There is supposedly something missing, so something external needs to be applied to fill these gaps and cracks in my psyche.

The manual used to classify mental illness, the DSM-V, neatly packages collections of symptoms using a diagnostic label. These diagnoses paint a picture of a distinguished identity based on how people are different from what has been defined as normal. Each diagnosis has with it a certain set of expectations and treatments. Once a diagnosis is established and used as the basis for therapy, we can become stuck thinking of ourselves only through the lens of that identity. My identity as a person who has been diagnosed with bipolar disorder is always with me, whether I am engaging in enlivening and enriching activity or wondering how I am going to make it through the day. This diagnostic label seems to overshadow all other aspects of my identity and personality; I can be a good person, but I am still a good person who has been diagnosed with bipolar disorder.

Many of the expectations that come along with mental health diagnoses are erroneous. We sometimes think: this person is schizophrenic; therefore, she is dangerous. That person is depressed; therefore, he is in need of my help. Another person is borderline; therefore, she couldn't possibly know how to be a good friend. Someone else is bipolar; therefore, he is unable to hold a job. These expectations create a false limitation on what each person is able to experience and achieve as a human being, and they can be internalized by the person who is experiencing mental illness — and therefore result in behaviors that are consistent with these limited ideas. I have imposed many of these limitations on myself, and breaking through them has been difficult because they are socially, culturally, and psychologically engrained within each of us in a different way.

Despite increasing public conversations about mental illness as well as widespread use of psychotropic medications, there is still a stigma associated with mental illness — not just in the United States where I live, but all around the world. People who are experiencing deep emotional pain too often suffer in silence because they feel ashamed to reveal to their friends and family, or even to a professional who remains a stranger, that they are in need of support. They may not want to be seen walking into a psychiatrist's office, or picking up a prescription at the pharmacy, when their neighbor might see them and wonder what is 'wrong' with them. Children might be told not to talk about their 'family problems' outside of the house, perpetuating the cycle of hiding in shame to cope with the social stigma of mental illness.

In my own life, I have sought external approval and even a sense of completion through others because I have been told over and over again in multiple situations that I am not good enough as I am. This has been reinforced by multiple professional opinions that have labeled me in a number of 'abnormal' ways. By focusing outside of myself for happiness, I have sacrificed my own intrinsic value. I have hidden or even altered who I really am to fit in and to be successful in social and professional situations. I have also numbed the pain of isolation and shame that comes along with this by using drugs and alcohol.

Our stories of mental illness, both related to our own lives and to the cultural and social circumstances in which we live, are incomplete. Stories evolve over time as a way to more deeply understand human nature and the meaning of life. They both clarify where we stand and have the potential to transform our lives. We have the power to rewrite the story of mental illness so that it serves our true needs and helps us heal. Because we or someone we love has a mental health diagnosis, our stories about it need to evolve so that we can all consistently be whole, happy, and healthy.

Mental illness is an integral part of who we are, but it doesn't define or limit us as human beings. Mental illness is an expression of our special exceptionality. The processes through which our cognitive and emotional systems interact creates a distinctive palette that we can use to paint the fabric of our lives. No two people with mental illness will experience it in quite the same way. My experience of bipolar disorder is unique to me and very different from how other people with this same dis-ease experience it.

Mental illness has caused great pain in my life, but it has also been a source of strength. The way my brain works is an asset that, in spite of sporadic setbacks, enriches my life. It has been a special gift that helps me thrive in complexity, appreciate diverse perspectives, creatively engage with challenges, and envision possibilities that might otherwise remain obscured. By being flexible and responsive, my mental illness has become a strong component of my mental acuity and resilience.

As an alternative to treating mental illness by evaluating and controlling it, we can also seek greater understanding and acceptance of our emotions to heal and thrive. Instead of judging ourselves and changing to meet other people's standards, we can discover and illuminate all of the greatness within so that we can shine the beautiful, warming light of a healthy mind and heart on the world.

Traditional approaches to treating mental illness aim to reduce symptoms and improve livelihood by suppressing or removing atypical emotions. My personal approach to healing has been to balance and harmonize my emotions instead. My sense of despair has helped me to develop strong and sincere empathy for others who are suffering. My anger has made me a activist who provokes personal and social change. By integrating my 'negative' emotions with my 'positive' emotions, I am able to bring my whole self into my life every day, rather than leave bits and pieces of it — which might actually be useful or even transformative — behind. I have learned to be productive and to meaningfully contribute to the world, and this has led to a great sense of purpose and fulfillment.

As a person who has been diagnosed with mental illness, I have felt a lot of pressure, unbearable at times, to both hide who I am and to change who I am. Rather than slash my inner self and mask the way I present myself to others, I now choose to be authentic and sincere instead. I am honest with myself and others about who I am, my thoughts and feelings, and my desires and dreams. We can heal and promote healing in others by being more of who we really, truly are. Our hearts want to sing a special song to share the intricacies and complexities of our existence. Our mind yearns to explore and expand into unknown territory. We can overcome the psychological and social oppression related to mental illness by simply enjoying the freedom of loving self-expression.

It may seem as though I am dismissing medical evaluation and treatment or other traditional means of care. I am not. While I have had some very negative experiences, and I know that others share in my disappointment and disillusionment, I also know that traditional treatment for mental illness saves lives. I still have hope that I will someday find a brilliant therapist who is just right for me and at times contemplate whether or not I should resume medication. If you are in treatment and it is working, don't stop. If you are in need of help, do not ever hesitate to reach out to a caring professional for assistance. Keeping an open heart and mind means that we can choose to include the opinions of helping professionals; however, we are not necessarily limited to those outsider perspectives.

With that being said, let's explore the meaning of happiness and how this relates to our understanding of mental illness.

Chapter Two
The Quest for Happiness

The way each person interprets the meaning of happiness is as unique as every manifestation of life on the planet. When you think about the word 'happy,' it likely invokes a certain emotional response which I can assure you is quite different from what your neighbor might be feeling when this particular word is used. It might make you think of other words such as joy, peace, contentment, pleasure, bliss, or amusement. Perhaps it provokes pleasant memories or inspiration for a better tomorrow. Like mental illness, the definition of happiness is complex, dynamic, and even nebulous. While there are many ways of defining and understanding the meaning of happiness, all of them are valid and complementary. Together, they create a full picture of something that all of us desire more of in our lives in one way or another.

Happiness is sometimes thought of as a trait. A trait is something with which we are born; in other words, some people have a lot of it and other people don't have very much at all. We don't have a lot of choice or control over our traits because they are gifted at birth. We can make the most of what we have, but the traits that have been entrusted to us are for the most part fixed and can't be further developed over time. While situations and our behavior may activate or influence our traits, ultimately they are automatic set points to which we return after these stimuli end. According to this type of theory, people who are mentally ill have a limited capacity to experience happiness because of the way our brains are hardwired. Happiness remains out of reach unless our brains can be chemically altered or retrained to work in a different way. This is unfortunately where some mental health treatment ends.

Conversely, happiness can be understood as a part of our personality. Our personality emerges from within but can evolve over time. It is shaped by relationships, circumstances, and life experiences. When our personality reflects an intrinsic sense of happiness, it shows through our word choice, tone of voice, body language, and ways of connecting with others. A person who has a cheerful disposition or a positive attitude is emanating her or his happy personality. Thinking of happiness as a component of our personality rather than as a trait offers two advantages: it connects this aspect of ourselves to the whole of our character, and it offers us some degree of flexibility and control over how we adapt to, and function in, the world. Mental illness, in this vein of thinking, reflects a deficit in our personality; however, because our personality is made up of the totality of our thoughts and feelings and the unique way that we express them, there is hope that we can make up for this deficit by choosing to strengthen and build upon other areas.

Happiness can also be thought of as an object, or a thing that exists outside of ourselves. According to this view, happiness is something we chase and try to both acquire and achieve. It becomes an intangible possession, or something we grasp and claim as a part of our personal identity. Because it is objectified, happiness can be accumulated, hoarded, and leveraged. The more happiness we have, the more power we supposedly possess. Unfortunately, when we chase after things they typically evade us and when we hold on too tight we can suffocate them. If happiness is a thing, then it is one that should be appreciated and savored rather than pursued and used. Mental illness, too, can be thought of as an object. Rather than pursuing mental illness, we usually try to box it up or run away from it away instead. We would easily give it away to another if only it were something desirable. As opposed to happiness, the more mental illness that we have, the worse off we are. We might seek happiness to crowd out or push away the mental illness in our lives. As our happiness increases, the hold of our mental illness decreases. When thought of as discrete objects, happiness and mental illness simply don't mix.

Happiness is also a feeling or emotion. As a feeling, it is something we experience in the moment while as an emotion it is something felt on a much deeper, more sustained level. Either way, like all feelings and emotions, it can be difficult to understand and to describe to others. In many sessions of talk therapy, when asked to describe my feelings and emotions, I have often felt unable to completely capture them with words. When I did finally find words to try to explain them, even with my background as a person who can be clever with language, I didn't quite seem able to adequately describe what was in my mind and my heart. If we have experienced little happiness in our lives, describing it with words can be even more daunting. Although explaining our feelings and emotions with words can be difficult, we can experience and express them in other ways so that we can become more aware of how they are impacting us. If we can't explain what happiness feels like using words, we can instead imagine the sensations we might feel in our body and the clarity and balance we might experience in our minds. We can also express the notion of happiness through art such as painting or dance in which words are not necessary. If happiness is a feeling or an emotion, we may be predisposed to have a certain base value of happiness or to experience happiness on a more consistent or erratic basis. Although much of our emotional response to the world is innate, it is heavily influenced by our circumstances, culture, choices, behavior, and relationships. Our emotional framework can shift and expand over time by intentionally becoming more aware of our feelings and making ongoing choices that redirect our emotional response in a way that creates more happiness, or less, in our lives.

Happiness can also be a skill, or something we learn to do through repeated practice. Writing, for me and most others, is a skill. I may have been born with a flavor for words, but my ability to write well has been developed throughout my life by continually practicing and expanding outside of my comfort zone by trying new topics and styles of writing. Similarly, we can develop our capacity to experience happiness through practice and application in different situations. As a person who experiences mental illness, there have been times in my life when I get stuck in a rut of negative thinking and behavior. A confrontation with someone that jeopardizes my sense of identity can result in weeks of obsessive rumination about what happened or what I would have liked to have happened instead. I could walk under a beautiful blue sky, hear exhilarating music, or meet the most kind and wonderful person in the world but it wouldn't matter because my thoughts would be stuck someplace else. To develop my happiness skill in circumstances such as these, I need to be aware of moments when I am not experiencing happiness and intercept whatever is causing me emotional pain so my thoughts and feelings can be directed to a more peaceful place. The more I practice applying happiness in moments of difficulty, the more consistently I will feel a sense of contentment and inner peace regardless of the circumstances in my life. Happiness is a muscle that grows when it is used. The more we feel a sense of happiness, the more we will want to experience it rather than something that causes us unnecessarily sustained pain and anguish.

Similarly, happiness can also be a repeated pattern of behavior. It is not just something we think or feel, but something we actively do in the world. Being happy means to act happy; not in a phony way, but in a sincere way that connects our innermost desires with what we do in our daily lives. As a person who suffers because of mental illness, I have too often acted out of anger or sadness — even when happiness could be found deep within my heart. I have also suppressed my desires to maintain a sense of stability in my life, only to find that I felt bored, frustrated, and restless as a result. We can become happier both in the moment and in general by allowing our passions the freedom to grow by taking steps to share and nurture them. People who are happy consistently act in ways that perpetuate a sense of happiness. When our actions result in more love and peace in the world, we are creating happiness not just within ourselves but for all others to enjoy as well. We are choosing to live in and co-create a happier and more loving world, and those behavioral choices are contagious.

In contrast to thinking of happiness as an object, or as something that can be acquired, happiness can alternatively be thought of as a process. It is something that emerges from moment to moment in our life journey. We experience happiness as we go about our daily lives; it ebbs and flows with our attention and intention. Happiness cannot be defined because it is always evolving, growing, and transforming. It is always with us as we search for meaning and for love. Recovery from the experience of mental illness, too, is a process. There is no specific point at which we will be 'cured' of our dis-ease. We may wish to function at a certain level in order to achieve a specific goal and to be able to sustain that level of achievement over time, but on the inside our search for happiness and fulfillment will continue. The happiness journey is traveled throughout life, until we completely give up or die.

Finally, happiness is also a sense of connection — to ourselves, others, the planet, and spirituality. It is knowing deep within that all of our thoughts, feelings, and actions have a magnificent consequence because everything is interconnected. When we are happy, we are connected to our life purpose and are able to discover and create abundant opportunities to share our special gifts with the world. Happiness revels in the curious joy of relationships, risking security to reveal the prosperity of love. We trust that we are loved, appreciated, and understood, and we easily love, appreciate, and understand others. Mental illness severs all of these connections. We feel cut off from others, at war with ourselves, and as though nothing we do will ever make a difference. Restoring internal and external connections and developing nurturing relationships feeds our happiness.

Happiness also has many different expressions, or ways of presenting itself in the world through human beings. Each of these expressions integrates the aforementioned forms and can be understood as static or dynamic, and as simple or complex. These expressions can be transitory or they can be sustaining and self-perpetuating. Every expression of happiness is important and life-enriching regardless of its depth or longevity. To simplify the many ways we express and experience happiness, I will explore seven types below: cheerfulness; pleasure; exhilaration; delight; resilience; contentment; and fulfillment. These types of happiness are powerful antidotes to the experience of mental illness; however, some are more potent than others. Their healing power depends on our unique mental-emotional composition and the circumstances under which we are experiencing pain. All of them have been useful to me at different times in my life as a means of coping with and transcending the anguish of mental illness.

Cheerfulness is a simple but very valuable expression of happiness. It is a lighthearted approach to engagement with life. Cheer is the outward manifestation of a kind and lovely inner self. Through cheer, we are able to reach out beyond ourselves to communicate with others in helpful and constructive ways. It is the ability to attract and flow with positivity and radiance. Cheer is based on an optimistic outlook where the goodness in everything is easily apparent. For me, being cheerful doesn't always feel natural. While there is definitely a great deal of cheerfulness inside of me, I am more often hard and distant. By tapping into my inner well of cheer, I can remove the barriers that separate me from others and trust that those relationships will be filled with mutual respect and kindness. Cheer helps me to enter relationships without judgment and with appreciation for the great beauty inside others. When other people react negatively to me, as they often do, I can remain connected to the cheerfulness inside of me and open myself up to new opportunities for relationships with others. Experiences such as these serve as gentle detours to redirect our energy in a more positive and enriching way.

Pleasure is the process of fulfilling our desires. When we experience pleasure, we are allowing ourselves to savor the many joys of being alive. We are intentionally following our passions and integrating them into our daily lives. Being filled with pleasure is to live a sensual life where colors, smells, sounds, tastes, and sensations combine to create beautiful and miraculous experiences that continue to ground and inspire us long after the moment has passed. Pleasure makes life more meaningful and valuable. I have had many pleasurable experiences that continue to positively influence my life today. The most powerful pleasurable experiences in my life have been the most simple. They include a few moments of quiet contemplation by the seaside on a pleasantly warm day, patiently waiting for a flower I planted to blossom, listening to a favorite song over and over again, eating a ripe peach and allowing the juice to run down my arms, and losing track of time because I got lost in a really good book. These simple pleasurable experiences are what make life worthwhile. A life without simple pleasures is sure to be unbearably dry, boring, and harsh. Making time for pleasure, and allowing myself to fully feel and enjoy pleasurable experiences, adds vibrancy to my life and this brightens the darkness that too often results from mental illness.

Exhilaration is perhaps a more exciting form of happiness. It is the reward we experience after taking a personal risk. It is a rush of adrenaline that follows great achievements or ecstatic experiences. Unlike cheer and pleasure, exhilaration comes in with a splash rather than remaining with us on a consistent level which might be exhausting (at least for most of us!). However, we can also experience exhilaration by continually facing the fear in our lives. Doing things that make us feel uncomfortable is essential for learning, opening ourselves up, and healing. Mental illness will persist in our lives unless we are able to courageously take a realistic look at what is going on inside of us. The terror we might feel when facing our mental illness is actually the excitement of new possibilities. When we push ourselves to go beyond the comfort of what is familiar to us, we will feel the sublime elation of personal growth.

Delight is a consistent enchantment with life. A delightful life is filled with delicate and intricate loveliness. With delight in our hearts, we can be in touch with the magnificent beauty of the world. We recognize that we are surrounded by the pure, unadulterated happiness of flowers, trees, the stars, waterfalls, and rainbows. At each moment, we are overflowing with appreciation and gratitude for the many gifts of being alive. Nothing can be taken for granted, because life is precious and perfect. When I feel overwhelmed because my mental illness has taken control of my life, it is often because I have lost sight of delight. My focus shifts to all of the heavy, burdensome, and unpleasant things in my life and I get stuck in a pattern of thinking and feeling in negative ways. I feel disconnected from the great beauty within me and around me, and forget to be grateful for the many ways this beauty enriches my life.

Resilience is another expression of happiness. Resilience is the ability to bounce back when we experience challenges in our life. During difficult moments, we can use resilience to return to our center and respond with agility. By remaining true to ourselves regardless of the circumstances we face, the happiness in our lives becomes more consistent. As we move on from difficult circumstances, drawing from an inner source of strength to guide us, we become better able to overcome similar challenges that the future might hold. Resilience not only helps us maintain a sense of equilibrium, it strengthens our inner core over time. When mental illness takes over, our purpose becomes buried in fear and anger. We are easily shaken and driven off course by even the smallest bump in the road. Our problems become the focus of our attention rather than our own needs and desires.

Contentment is a serene sense of ease and grace. It is a peaceful, trusting joy that fills our minds and hearts. When we are content, we feel blissful and free. Contentment is a state of natural well-being where we languish in all of the still resting spaces of our hearts. Mental illness often results in an overwhelming feeling of discontent with life. Not only does mental illness make everything seem problematic and difficult, but the dis-ease itself is undesirable. We are typically told that the best way to heal from mental illness is to change our minds and our feelings; however, this results in continual dissatisfaction with ourselves and with life in general. The more we try to become happy, the less happy we really, truly are.

Fulfillment is much deeper than contentment; it is a continual alignment with, and integration of, our purpose and passions in life. It is to live a life full of meaning and significance. Our mental, emotional, and spiritual energies are consistently directed toward our life purpose. We continually nurture our truest nature, honoring the greatness within. We can certainly live a fulfilling life with, or even because of, mental illness; however, it can diminish our ability to recognize the most important things in our lives. Feeding our mental illness with energy that could otherwise be used for our fulfillment can be exhausting and depleting. This is a vicious cycle that sucks up more and more of our energy and it can be difficult to escape.

We typically act in ways that increase the amount of happiness, or decrease the amount of pain, in our lives. We seek all of the types of happiness explored above in a number of different ways. Some are helpful and healthy while others can be draining and destructive. By identifying and exploring the various means of attempting to become happier, we can carefully choose those that best serve our needs.

Compromise is one tool we use to become happier. When we compromise, we give something up to obtain something else that is desirable. The loss is typically deemed to be smaller than the gain that is achieved, or the gain is so important that the loss seems insignificant in comparison. We compromise both within ourselves and in our relationships. Recovery from mental illness is often a game of compromise; through trial and error we determine which parts of ourselves to give up, and how much needs to be sacrificed, to feel better from day to day. We also compromise with our loved ones for the good of the relationship; we let something go so that we can communicate peacefully and live more harmoniously with others.

We also try to become happier through manipulation. We manipulate ourselves by attempting to control our thoughts and feelings and by redefining their meaning in a way that heightens happiness. We also bargain with ourselves, offering little rewards when we achieve something that moves us closer to our happiness goal. Manipulation becomes more problematic in relationships. When we try to control other people and bend them toward our own needs and purposes, we unfairly violate the privilege of the relationship. Having a mental illness does not give us the right to expect others to do what we want them to do for our own personal benefit. We can offer others our love, and hope that they will love and understand us in return, but we cannot selfishly demand that others put our needs before their own.

Hoarding is another means of seeking happiness. We acquire and accumulate things that extend and enhance our personal identity. Purchasing things we don't need does not necessarily mean that we are hoarding; when we buy things that are useful and that add value to our lives, we are purposefully spending our money. But when those things are not used, or if their maintenance requires more energy that we feel willing to use for that purpose, then we are hoarding. My closet is full of clothing that I hardly ever wear and a few pieces that I will likely never wear again. Having a lot of clothes gives me a sense of control and choice that I do not always feel in other parts of my life. Yet having these excess items is also an emotional drain; the clutter they create is an extension of the clutter in my mind.

Compulsive and addictive behavior is another means of seeking happiness. Like hoarding, these behaviors can be an attempt to cultivate a false sense of control. We take an action to intentionally suppress or escape from a part of ourselves in order to achieve a desired result. Sustaining these results requires more and more suppression of, or escaping from, our self. Compulsions and addictions typically bring a sense of happiness that is false and fleeting rather than fulfilling.

We can also seek happiness through sharing. When we share ourselves with others, we create more happiness in the world through resonance and affirmation. Our ideas, time, space, and things we make all add value to our lives as well as the lives of our friends, family, and neighbors. There are many ways that we can share our gifts with the world; we can share our talents with a charitable organization that is dear to our hearts, lovingly create an exquisite — or delightfully simple — meal for a friend, or post a novel idea on the Internet so that others may benefit from our wisdom.

Another way of finding happiness, and in my view the best way, is through loving. When we genuinely love ourselves and others, happiness will easily find us. It really is that simple.

We can put together the types and expressions of happiness as well as the means of pursuing them to become more aware of our motivation. To heighten our awareness and explore possibilities, we can ask ourselves questions such as: What does happiness mean to me? What is it that I really want? What am I doing to create more of that in my life? Is it working? After contemplating these questions, you can develop your own definition and course of action.

Happiness isn't just something we do, or something we become if we do certain things — it is something that we are without intervention. We treat happiness as though it is yet one more thing to be achieved when really it is our purest and most natural state of being. We can release a life full of pain and suffering and lovingly accept one that is effortless, flowing, and free.

We are happy when we are aware of, and fully immersed in, the present moment. We can allow ourselves to experience peace, joy, rapture, and bliss from moment to moment. Being stuck in the past or eagerly anticipating a better future diminishes our ability to be happy right now. Ruminating about past experiences keeps us stuck there; this makes it difficult to open up to the happiness that is imminently available to us. Obsessively thinking about the future shifts our focus away from the reality of what we are currently experiencing physically, mentally, and emotionally to what we imagine or hope we might experience at some point in the future. While it is helpful and important to make sense of our past experiences and to plan for and anticipate the future, when we do so at the expense of appreciating what we are experiencing right now we miss out on so much happiness. Looking back or thinking ahead to distance ourselves from our suffering also detaches us from opportunities for happiness in the present moment.

Much of our ability to experience happiness is influenced by our perceptions. Perception is the way we experience and understand our experiences, our relationships, and our world through our senses, mind, and hearts. Our perceptions represent the intersection and interaction of our senses, intuition, intellect, and emotion — revealing a unique complexity that naturally unfolds from person to person, situation to situation, and moment to moment. An intricate, personal code is established over time as we interpret and make sense of our life experiences and discover themes. Those themes and their meanings evolve as we mature. But they can sometimes become engrained, and when that happens our ability to learn, grow, and experience wellness becomes stifled — particularly if our perceptions have been strongly influenced by imbalanced emotions.

This book will explore twelve *perception re-conceptions*, or ways we can rethink and rebirth the way we understand the world. Each perception re-conception represents a theme that has emerged from my own experience of transcending the social and mental traps of mental illness to live a life full of happiness and meaning. You may find that many of these themes are also applicable to your life, or you may not. Either way, coming along with me on this journey of self-exploration will help you to discover, describe, redefine, and expand your own perceptual themes so that you too can experience more peace and fulfillment.

The twelve perception re-conceptions that have had the most meaning in my life, which I will share with you throughout this book, are:

- **Occupation to liberation of the mind** — releasing negativity, limiting beliefs, and assumptions;

- **Probability to possibility** — creatively constructing our emotional landscape;

- **Isolation to integration** — discovering internal unity and appreciating the interconnectedness of all things;

- **Immobility to fluidity** — becoming unstuck and flowing through life;

- **Rigid to responsive** — softening and opening up;

- **Austerity to simplicity** — creating clarity by releasing mental and emotional waste;

- **Critique to compassion** — accepting and loving our self and others;

- **Full to empty** — cleansing our hearts and minds to make choices that add value;

- **Fragile to delicate** — allowing ourselves to be sensitive and vulnerable;

- **Depletion to pollination** — generously sharing to enrich our lives and the world;

- **Dreaming to being** — integrating thoughts and desires with action and results; and

- **Life is strife to life is love** — surrendering to the power of love.

Each of the following twelve chapters will explore these perception re·conceptions in more detail, offering stories and specific suggestions to make simple but profound changes to restore emotional balance in our lives. As you read through each chapter, think about how the ideas shared might apply to your unique beliefs, needs, and circumstances. Develop a plan to integrate some of the concepts into your daily life. More importantly, identify your own perceptual map and start redesigning and expanding it so that you can discover and experience your most fulfilling life journey.

Chapter Three
Perception Re-conception #1:
From Occupation to Liberation of the Mind

People who experience mental illness are too often oppressed in our culture and society. We are misunderstood, manipulated, and excluded. Yet, the oppression we experience by others pales in comparison to that which we unintentionally impose upon ourselves. When we choose to limit the possibilities in our lives because of our mental illness, or decide that we have a limited capacity to think, feel, or do what we desire, we have relinquished our emotional freedom. If our minds become occupied by mental illness in this way, we can liberate our thoughts and feelings through awareness and intentionality.

Emotions that we typically think of as negative, such as anger and fear, serve a real purpose in our lives. Anger can help us process our grief or channel our energy and fear can protect us from harm. Unfortunately, our minds can hang on to and become occupied by these negative emotions even when their purpose has passed. When we get stuck in this way, it becomes difficult to truly enjoy our lives. Happiness becomes more and more elusive when our minds are overwhelmed by negative emotions. Some of the negative emotions that have stayed with me include anger, worry, fear, guilt, and shame. While all of these feelings emerged in response to circumstances and experiences in my life, those circumstances and experiences have shifted and passed. The feelings associated with what has previously happened in my life are still alive within me despite their diminished utility.

Anger is something that I struggle with on almost a daily basis. I am angry about the many unjust experiences that I have had throughout my life as well as those that I have observed in the lives of others. My anger stems from a yearning for what might have been, but wasn't, and strong feelings that I or others have been unfairly disadvantaged by certain life experiences and circumstances. While I also acknowledge and understand that these challenges have been opportunities to learn and strengthen my resolve, there is still a strong sense of loss, remorse, and resentment. My anger is directed at those who cause harm and the society that allowed them to get away with what they did; however, I am even angrier at myself because I have at times allowed these experiences to stifle my spirit and suspend my momentum. I am easily angered by mere infractions because there is so much anger within me and it is easily tapped. Luckily for me, and for the rest of the world, I have been able to effectively channel my anger into activism. Rather than thinking of myself as a victim, I have found solidarity in the suffering of others and have worked diligently to help us all overcome the difficulties that we face in our lives.

I obsessively worry about a lot of things. I am constantly counting anything related to my money and my weight — two areas of insecurity rooted in my childhood. Even though I have, in general, gained self-acceptance in these areas, my obsessive thoughts persist. While logically the amount of my worry might have decreased in proportion to the difference between my reality and my aspiration, it has in fact only steadily increased and compounded over time. The more I worry, the more I worry. I do not only worry about those two things; my life is fraught with anxiety in nearly every area. With everything I do or plan to do at some point in the future, I automatically imagine the worst and unsuccessfully try to prevent my fears from being realized by thinking through (that is, obsessing about) the various possible outcomes of the situation.

Fear is closely tied to worry for me, and it has prevented me from doing many things that I have felt called to do throughout my life. I am terrified of making a mistake, failure, feeling or appearing inadequate, dying, being in unbearable pain for an extended period of time, and being exposed as a phony — among many other things. My fears are obviously pervasive and irrational. All of these fears are connected to a deep sense of insecurity; perhaps keeping them around in my mind gives me something familiar and strangely comforting on which I can hang.

I also carry around a lot of guilt. I feel guilty about things I did and said as well as things I should have done and said but did not. Not only do I feel guilty about my actions, or lack thereof; I also sometimes feel guilty about the many good things in my life. Because I have such a strong sense of equity, which is very much rooted in experiences and awareness of both privilege and deprivation, I often think about how my lot in life compares to other people's circumstances. Guilt looms over me like a cloud about to burst open with a ravaging storm, and it follows me through both good and bad times.

Shame is a much deeper sense of despair not related to anything over which I have control, but rather the essence of who I am as a human being. My shame calls into question the very validity of my continued existence. It is tied to deteriorated self-esteem and a distorted perception of who I am. Often, my shame relates to the disparity between what I am currently experiencing — emotionally, experientially, and physically — and the kind of life I think I ought to be living.

I not only allowed anger, worry, fear, guilt, and shame to visit; I have rolled out the red carpet and invited them to stay. As a result, all of these negative emotions have become trapped in my mind. They are swarming around, building nests, and squatting in places that ought to be reserved for joy, love, and peace. They have created congestion and confusion, impacting my ability to think and feel with clarity.

Allowing these negative emotions to occupy my mind has been both a seductive path and a slippery slope. These feelings are deceptively alluring because they make me feel as though I am actively processing or addressing my challenges and working toward changing my life. This false sense of security provokes the perpetuation of those feelings. Yet, they never really help me to move forward. In fact, they push me further and further behind. When I allow myself to be seduced by negative emotions, I get sucked into the quicksand of negative spirals, sinking deeper and deeper.

Like happiness, we seek and cling to negativity because it seems to fill some immediate need and, at least in the short run, relieve our pain. Allowing ourselves to feel these emotions may in fact be healing and transformative. But when negative emotions overwhelm us, define us, and become a part of our identity, then it has gone too far.

When this happens, our negative emotions become mental debts. Mental debts are deficits that we carry around within us from previous experiences. They multiply over time, becoming more and more intense and destructive. The benefit of a mental debt, as opposed to a financial debt, is that it can be paid off at any time. By focusing our attention and our intention, we can move through and past negativity so that our emotions become more balanced. We can gain the perspective needed to understand that negative emotions have a place, but that they are not enough for us to transcend our challenges. Negativity can retain its ability to be used as a form of currency in our healing process, but when combined with hope, inner peace, and self-love, its value is amplified.

The space in our minds is precious and should be cherished. We too easily allow negative emotions to take over and control an excessive amount of this space. A balanced approach that integrates both negative and positive emotions will help us to release the hold of our mental illness.

We can intentionally loosen the grip that our negative emotions have on us through a four-step process. The four steps in this process are acknowledgement, acceptance, surrender, and letting go. By easing into and through these four steps, our negative emotions will be free to circulate in and out of our minds as needed rather than serving as a crutch upon which we base the full weight of our troubles.

The first step is to acknowledge that negative emotions exist within us. To acknowledge the feelings that are occupying our mind, we need to become more aware of their presence and the impact they have on our lives. During this phase, we not only realize that these feelings exist, we also become better able to name and describe them at any moment. It is a continual process of being aware of our feelings and choosing to be honest with ourselves about what is going on in our minds.

The second step is acceptance. Rather than judging our feelings, which perhaps only leads to more negativity, we can accept them for what they are. We can realize that these emotions are there for a reason, to fill a real need, and that we have done our best to use them to our advantage regardless of the results. We are accepting both the emotions themselves and our own desire to attract and retain them.

Next, we can lovingly surrender to all of the struggles in our mind. During this step, we decide that we no longer need to control these negative emotions and that they no longer need to control us. Rather than continuing to be at war with ourselves and with our feelings, we can allow the feelings to exist within us without attachment. We are dislodging them from our psychic grip and allowing them to remain inside of us, but not as a part of our identity.

Finally, we can release the negative emotions and set them free. During this final phase of this transformative process, we see how our thoughts and feelings exist separate from us, and how they can easily enter and exit our minds and hearts. Our negative emotions remain available to us as a valuable tool when needed, but we no longer feel compelled to rely on them during challenging times. We can fully let go of them and let them out of our sight, knowing that at the slightest call they will be available and come running back to us.

Our mind adapts to the social environment in which we live so that we can successfully interact and flourish within its conditions. To function in society, our mind is ordered, tamed, and suppressed regardless of whether or not we suffer from mental illness. When we do have a mental illness, the adaptation process is even more complicated because we are also compensating for our mental and emotional differences. Through the four-step process of releasing the negative emotions that occupy our mind, we can become more aware of how our feelings originate and develop over time; we can also become more agile in responding to our environment in a healthy and productive way.

We typically think of our minds as being organized into neat and discrete categories. These mental shortcuts help us to more quickly process and make sense of information. We develop a complex filing system in our heads so that if a particular word or object is recalled a complete dossier of information becomes available to us. As we continue to have more life experiences, those files grow thick with additional details and nuance. While there may be an elaborate cross-referencing system in place, each piece of information is filed away in a specific place where it can be pulled out when we need to investigate something.

Alternatively, we can think of our minds as a complex system of networks. Each bit of information exists independently, has the ability to easily move around, and is infinitely interconnected with all of the other bits of information that exist within our minds. As we experience life, new connections among all of these bits are developed and strengthened. As opposed to the filing system that we typically associate with our minds, this network is creative and evolving with unlimited possibilities for reorganization. Our capacity to understand ourselves and the world becomes more fluent and our ability to adapt to the environment becomes more fluid.

Regardless of whether we view our minds as a group of files or a system of networks, we may still hold many assumptions and limiting beliefs that impede mental and emotional liberation. These assumptions and limiting beliefs are judgments about ourselves and the world that emerge when we understand everything in relation to a normalized standard.

Let's look at the example of bipolar disorder. I have held a lot of limiting beliefs and assumptions related to this mental illness throughout my life. A list of specific criteria is used to make this diagnosis. If I have experienced a certain number of items on this list, then I can assume that I am afflicted with this dis-ease. I can therefore also assume that there is something wrong with me, that I need to change in order to be healthy, and that I am in need of help to do so. I can also assume that I will have certain feelings or experiences such as deep sadness, rage, misery, elation, and/or rapid mood swings. In addition to these assumptions, I might also have certain limiting beliefs such as, 'I am inadequate as I am,' or 'I will never be able to function without the assistance of medication.' I might even blame my mental illness when things go wrong in my life. When relationships sour, I might think that I have been misunderstood and underappreciated because of my difference. When I have poor job performance, I can justify that by explaining that I do not have the ability to control my emotions.

These are all examples of how my mind has become occupied by the assumptions and limiting beliefs that are commonly associated with my mental health diagnosis. If I had chosen the simple filing approach, where everything is placed in a folder in a neat little box, there would be no possibility for convergence with new and better ways of interpreting the meaning of my life. In contrast, I can identify the things I am feeling and experiencing and note that they fit into the pattern that has been labeled as bipolar disorder. But this is only the beginning, not the ending, of my self-discovery. From there, I can look closely at each symptom — its source and its impact on my life — and then zoom out to see the comprehensive picture of who I am as a human being. During this process of investigation, I will likely uncover new connections that would otherwise go unnoticed. I might see that my enduring despair is deeply connected to a sense of empathy or that my unpredictable shifts in mood make me more resilient in, and excited about, the rapidly changing world in which we live. Each symptom can be dissected and combined with other aspects of who I am to develop a new way of understanding myself. And this understanding can grow and evolve over time as I become more deeply aware of the meaning and purpose of my life. My mind becomes liberated and free to transform into ever more beautiful and intricate arrangements.

Metaphor is another powerful means of liberating our thoughts and feelings. A metaphor is a description of what we are experiencing through the example of an unrelated object that has a symbolic meaning. My previous example of thinking of our minds as a filing cabinet is one example of a metaphor. Through metaphor, we can expand and deepen our self-understanding, and shift the ways we perceive the world.

One of my favorite metaphors to understand any aspect of life is that of the theater. Our mind is like a theater, with regular rehearsals and performances. Through the metaphor of the theater, we can learn new ways to liberate our thoughts and feelings.

Our minds are filled with words that combine to form scripts. These scripts can emerge in response to unique circumstances, but they can also be something that repeatedly enters our minds without an invitation. Some of the scripts that might occupy our minds include: 'I hope I do well at work today,' 'she hates me,' 'I'm fat,' 'this is going to suck,' 'I'm going to mess this up,' 'I hate myself,' 'I'm stuck in my life,' 'I don't care,' or 'I will never be successful.' Scripts such as these that occupy our minds are highly dramatic and are truly damaging to our self-esteem.

Fortunately, we are the author of our own scripts as well as the director and producer of our internal theatrical productions. We have the ability to control the specific words that enter our minds, how they are used, their intonation, and what meaning we associate with them. We can also control the frequency of each script being repeated. Imagine how boring it would be to go to a play and watch an actor repeat the same sentence over and over again. You would want your money back! Yet, we subject ourselves to this torture inside our anxious minds without thinking twice.

As the author of our minds, we can intentionally construct scripts that are empowering and enlivening. To begin, we need to be aware of the thoughts that pass through our minds so that we can change them. Think about some of the words that are most frequently used in your mental script. If you use a lot of words like hate, bored, or should have, then you are likely causing harm to yourself with your thoughts. Make a list of nurturing words that you could use, such as love, excited, or will, and weave them into your script on a consistent basis until they become your go to words. Tell yourself beautiful, lovely stories that prepare you to live a life filled with joy.

Your scripts likely include other characters; those characters can be mentioned as a part of your interior monologue or you might even offer those characters some dialogue. Be vigilant about who you let into your play; only allow characters to have a part if they are going to add value to your performance and enrich your life. In other words, our thoughts about others should be limited to those that significantly improve the quality of the script.

Not only are we the authors of our minds, we are also the audience. When we go to a play or movie as a spectator, we take in all of the sights and sounds and this arouses provocative thought and feeling. As the audience of our mental performance, certain ideas and emotions are inspired within us as we watch and listen. Because our mental theater is quite intimate, we, as the audience, can give nonjudgmental, loving feedback to ourselves, as the author, so that each performance is enhanced. We need not be a passive audience, nor one that is critical. Over time, with intentionality and purposeful engagement, our scripts and performances can become eloquent, refreshing, and transformative. We can control what happens in our minds and how we make meaning of our experiences.

In addition to the theater, there are many more metaphors that can be used to describe our minds. The metaphor that most deeply resonates with how we view ourselves reveals a lot about our internal belief system. We can also apply new metaphors to expand our self-understanding. Let's explore a few possible metaphors and their meaning: prison, a maze, a farm, an ocean, the sky, a forest, and the sun.

Our mind as a prison is a scary and confining space. We consistently punish ourselves for things that we once did. We subject ourselves to rigid routines and excessive discipline. We may desire freedom, but there is no way out — we are trapped. No matter what we do or say, we will remain isolated and restrained. Our mind is dark, cold, and barren.

It is easy to get lost in a maze. When we think of our minds as mazes, nothing feels familiar or safe. Everything looks the same and the monotony is confusing — possibly even maddening. We are alone and constantly in search of an exit, which is always just around the corner. We might become even more frustrated when we hear our peers giggling with joy because they have found the end of the maze while we remain lost somewhere in the middle. Hope and happiness surround us and seem to be just beyond our reach.

A farm looks idyllic from the outside, but it is excruciatingly difficult to maintain. The hard work it takes to run the farm is gratifying, but it is never-ending. We can choose what we sow and how much loving attention we give each of our plants and each of these factors will impact our harvest. Similarly, we can weed out anything invasive that might interfere with our bounty. In our minds, our thoughts are seeds that, when nurtured and given energy, grow over time. The weeds in our mind sap energy from the many potential blossoms within. The farm will ultimately flourish, but it takes time and a lot of hard work (and a little luck).

We can also think of our minds as an ocean. Various forms of life co-exist in the ocean. Some are nourishing, like seaweed, while others can be deadly (yet essential to the ecosystem), like sharks. An ocean is usually calm and peaceful, but it can be turbulent at times. The ocean draws people because of its serenity but every once in a while it causes great devastation. The ocean is always in motion and continually renewing, washing to shore its waste.

The sky is vast, open, and full of possibilities. Depending on how we position ourselves, it may seem bigger or smaller. The sky shares the illumination of the stars and the sun. It gently twinkles in the evening and beams during the day. The sky also presents beautiful sunrises and sunsets for all to see. It shows us lovely cloud formations that float in and out throughout the day. The sky sometimes opens up and unleashes a storm. Storms nourish our land, but they can also cause irreparable damage.

The forest is thick with vegetation. It is filled with old, sturdy tress as well as new growth. The forest is a magical place filled with mystery. The space can be a little dark, but the sun usually peaks through the leaves. We can easily become lost in the forest, because like the maze everything can look very similar. Unlike a maze, which is very orderly and patterned, the forest is more natural and organically emerges.

We can also think of our minds as a sun. The sun is warm and bright. It illuminates everything in its vicinity. The sun is a source of life. It is very hot and its rays can be blinding, so it is necessary to create space around it. We look forward to seeing the sun every morning. It is reliable and shows up without fail.

I see myself as a combination of all of these metaphors, and more. It is fun to explore the organization of our minds, and the meaning of the thoughts within them, in this way. You might have a totally different way of interpreting your mind. Perhaps you are a flower, a computer, a shoe, or a Pegasus. However you see yourself, metaphor can help us discover the power of our minds to heal. This power is liberating and can remain with us as we explore and balance our emotions on a daily basis.

We can also liberate our minds by removing mental barriers. Mental barriers provide contours for our perceived life possibilities. They can be controlling, numbing, and even paralyzing. Imagine walking one hundred miles through a field only to find a large fence that you are unable to climb. We construct these barriers in our minds all of the time. We tell ourselves that we can only go so far or be so much when in reality a whole field of possibilities lies beyond that fence. When we identify and remove the barriers in our minds, releasing everything within us that is oppressive, our most pure and beautiful self can emerge.

All of these tools can be used to create liberating emotional and mental clarity. When we identify and remove all of the thoughts and feelings that occupy our minds and our hearts, we can create space for more goodness and love in our lives. The pure ecstatic joy of true liberation will fill our hearts, and we will be able to experience perfectly peaceful contentment at any moment.

Chapter Four
Perception Re-conception #2:
From Probability to Possibility

Assumptions guide many aspects of our lives, regardless of our mental health status. It is natural to draw conclusions and to make predictions based on past experience or the wisdom of our elders. This minimizes our immediate anxiety and helps us feel more prepared to encounter whatever might happen in the future. With all of the many uncertainties of life, we can feel more secure knowing that some things will never change; they are constants that collectively create a map to guide us through the winding, rocky roads on the foggy evenings of our lives. Assumptions offer us protection and a sense of certainty in the midst of ambiguity.

Our assumptions provide us with a theoretical basis that we draw upon as we anticipate the future. It is unscientific theory, but grounded in the patterns we have discovered through our complex understanding of the experiences, thoughts, and feelings that we have had over time. As we age, our assumptions may change, contract, or expand in response to exposure to new ideas and experiences as well as through deeper connection to our emotions and their meaning.

In the late 1990s, I earned a business degree from a Catholic University. In addition to taking many business classes, I also studied philosophy and theology to round out my faith-based liberal arts education. As you might imagine, values such as rationality and absolutism were engrained in the curriculum. While I respectfully challenged many of the specific ideas that we were taught, upon reflection it is apparent to me that my education helped me to create a more orderly mind and life. I could identify and dissect all of the inputs and outputs that both contributed to the quality of my life and defined my identity.

In graduate school, at least for the first four years, my rational mind was reinforced through additional exposure to theories and practices that further promoted and even rewarded a formulaic, input-output style of thinking. I was developing the ability to predict the future with great acuity, and this gave me a sense of greater control in my life: if I do this, then that will *probably* happen. Or so I thought.

I now realize that relying on probability assumptions to inform my daily activities and life decisions can be highly problematic and prohibitive. Predictions about the future based on random life experiences from the past accordingly return random results. It is impossible to know with certainty what will happen as a result of what we think or do and, more importantly, why these things will happen. And that is one of the key points of our all too short lives — opening up to possibilities rather than relying on probabilities helps us to learn and form new cognitive, emotional, and spiritual connections. We aren't necessarily meant to know and control the future; releasing our reliance on predictions promotes the expansion of our perceptions as well as the ability to think more clearly and feel with greater depth as we ease into each moment with grace.

When we assume probability, we are admitting that we don't really know the whole truth. We *probably* know, but that doesn't mean that we know for sure. We are making an educated guess, with some degree of certainty, based on hunches and semi-scientific data derived from our observations. Our focus is on what we think we know, and hope that we can control, and this overshadows the unknown, which is nebulous and chaotic. That unknown is the possible — that beautiful, mysterious potential that too often escapes our attention.

Probability can be used to predict the outcome of a situation or to deduce the cause of that outcome. For example, I might think to myself (or say out loud), "I will probably make a mistake during my presentation at work. I will probably get nervous and forget what I wanted to say." Our use of the probability concept may not be so explicit. "I suck at making speeches. I can never remember my lines." These statements represent generalizations that have predictive power.

And guess what? If we predict failure for ourselves, we are *probably* going to fail! Probability is a losing game with no end in sight. We deserve better and owe it to ourselves to instead open up to what might be possible.

But sometimes we live our lives as if a possibility is a probability. I live in a Victorian house that, like most older homes, breathes very well. This provides an opportunity for little creatures to find their way into my home more often than I would like. Each year, when the tulips are in bloom and everything else seems as if it is right in the world as it only does on beautiful spring days, the panic begins to emerge. At any given moment, a bat could come swooping down toward me. And then it could fly away and hide in my closet. And then I might not find it for three days. And then I wouldn't be able to sleep. And then it might bite one of my cats. Or it could bite me. And then I could get rabies. And then my life would literally be over. Probably. Bats may play a very important role in our ecosystem, but in my home, their utility is very much underappreciated.

It is *possible* that a bat could find its way into my house at any moment. But since I only have up to three such visitors each year (and some years I don't have any), it definitely isn't *probable*. My anxiety, which returns every night for about five months out of the year, does not serve me well. It does not make me more prepared to evict a bat should one find their way into my house and it doesn't prevent them from entering. It just detracts from my well-being.

Whenever we believe something will probably happen, or something will probably cause a particular result, or that our hunches and beliefs are probably true, we forsake the opportunity to truly appreciate and enjoy what could be possible. We also get stuck with a behavior, thought, or action that causes us unnecessary pain and suffering.

If we experience delusions and hallucinations and accept them as the truth, then we are treating them as probabilities rather than possibilities. Yet, they are but one possible interpretation of reality. Similarly, the phenomenon of mental illness can be experienced and understood in multiple ways. There are many possibilities beyond what we automatically believe to be the probable truth.

Looking back, I can remember many times throughout my life when my mental health diagnosis consumed my identity. My thoughts, feelings, and behavior — particularly those that deviated from the norm — could all be explained by my diagnosis. My diagnosis could also be used as an excuse for inappropriate behavior because, as it is too often assumed, people who experience bipolar disorder are more likely to do all sorts of deviant things.

In that last sentence, I made the assumption that bipolar disorder was the cause of my thoughts and behavior, and therefore by extension anyone else who experiences bipolar disorder (or any group of people who share a diagnosis) can be expected to think and act in a similar manner. This can become a self-fulfilling prophecy for those of us who have a diagnosis. Sometimes we also exaggerate our symptoms, intentionally or not, to get the help we need. If we do not exhibit the predicted thought patterns and behaviors, then we lose that core component of our identity along with our ability to anticipate and control what will happen in the future. Because this loss can seem too great to bear, when we are so misunderstood in a world that seems to antagonize any form of difference, we sometimes subconsciously internalize and then act out those predictions about mental illness that we have absorbed from our culture, approaches to treatment, the expectations of others, and our own limited perceptions about our dis-ease.

Mental illness is not necessarily the cause of our thoughts, feelings and behavior; it is a contributing factor along with things like our environment, social and economic status, personality, support network, exposure to trauma, and cultural background. The degree to which mental illness diminishes our well-being varies from person to person, and within each person from moment to moment. While mental illness may influence how we think, what we feel, and what we do — and that influence may be very strong at times — it is just one of many things that come together to shape our human experience and the personal meaning that we attribute to those experiences. The impact of mental illness in our lives can be healthier and promote the fulfillment of our potential when we reject the idea that a diagnosis can or should be used to define or explain who we are in favor of the notion that it is one of many interrelated parts our being — and that it can lead to beautiful possibilities in our lives, not just very dismal probabilities.

Earlier in the book I described mental health diagnoses as labels. In this chapter, I explained how a mental health diagnosis can become part of our identity. Fortunately, our identity is not static and evolves over time as we are exposed to new ideas and experiences. Who we chose to be in the past does not define who we must be in the future. Sometimes we need to lose our identity to find ourselves — our true selves.

Labels and identity are intertwined. Our identity consists of multiple labels which taken together make us the unique, special person that we are. Mother. Athlete. Feminist. World Traveler. Survivor. Librarian. Superhero. Labels vary in their subjectivity; while mother is fairly (but not necessarily) straightforward, the phrase 'older mother' can mean different things to different people. The threshold, or cutoff point, where a person becomes an 'older mother' is an interpretive guess. Mental illness, too, is a label that is highly subjective. What degree of emotional anguish constitutes mental illness? What is the tipping point? And what does it truly mean to be mentally ill? What is probable for people who experience mental illness? What is possible? The answers to these questions will vary from person to person, from professional helper to professional helper, and from me to you.

This subjectivity gives us a lot of room for self-exploration. If we previously understood that our mental illness *probably* meant that we didn't have a chance in this world, there is *probably* someone else out there — and maybe many people — who disagree! If our mental illness leads us to believe that we are *probably* the answer to the world's prayers, then guess what? That is only one perspective — and one that is likely not held by most people. The truth is that we are all important, we all matter, we all have something to contribute, and we can never give up the quest to discover and rediscover our purpose.

Exploring and playing with possibilities is a lot more fun and interesting than predicting with probabilities. A probability prohibits our ability to adapt as well as our creativity and resilience. Possibilities, on the other hand, represent an endless number of opportunities that can keep us indefinitely engaged in the process of fully living our lives.

You are likely reading this book because a mental health diagnosis has been bestowed upon you. Or perhaps you know or love someone who fits that description. Along with that diagnosis came many prescribed probabilities related to emotional, mental, and behavioral capabilities. Hopefully, you carefully evaluated each of these before deciding to accept them. They may be true for you, but not necessarily.

Labeling or categorizing our thoughts, feelings, and behaviors can be helpful as a first step to self-understanding. Doing this is a critical tool to help us make sense of our experience. But if we stop there, this limited view of ourselves may be harmful. When we categorize, compartmentalize, and compare, we lose the gifts of our uniqueness and openness to interpretation that can provide a more robust basis for happiness and fulfillment. Mental health diagnoses can unintentionally define, confine, and constrain who we believe ourselves to be rather than open up special possibilities for our lives.

Mental illness is not rational, so it cannot be fully understood in a rational way. It is messy, chaotic, mysterious, and terrifying at times. But when we try to control it, it in fact controls us. When we attempt to push it away or hide it, it consumes us. When we get really honest with ourselves and intentionally abandon the pretense of this predicament, our loveliest authenticity will emerge and this, collectively, will help to end the stigma that surrounds mental illness in our society.

Using labels to describe ourselves conceals much of our character. Imagine placing a label on a jar of freshly cooked blackberry jam. You would know that it is blackberry jam because it says so on the label, not because you have thoroughly examined the contents of the jar. You have sadly just missed out on a lot of ooey, gooey goodness! If I stick a bipolar disorder (or any other) label on myself or someone else, I would similarly be hiding the rich nuance of my or that other person's existence. This is why I typically say, "I have experienced bipolar disorder" or "I have been diagnosed with bipolar disorder" rather than "I have bipolar disorder" or, even worse, "I am bipolar." There are thousands of labels that I could potentially choose for myself and it seems unfair to advantage one at the expense of so many others.

Rather than slapping a label on ourselves, we can instead bravely delve into our depths, explore all of the twists and turns in our minds, and work hard to discover and uncover our many layers. These layers build up over time, sometimes becoming entangled with others, presenting a complex and resistant web that strongly influences who we think we are or ought to be. Many of these layers protect us from the harshness of the world, while others block us from the rare beauty that can be found everywhere if we only look closely enough. As we explore these layers, we can better understand how they got there, why we hung onto them, the purpose they are serving — or the purpose we intended them to serve even though they truly aren't, and the potential utility of keeping that layer intact. As we go deeper and deeper, examining layer after layer, we can develop a comprehensive picture of how they all fit together to create the barriers and openings that have been constructed over time between us and the rest of the world.

Because we have so many layers, and these layers are intertwined and fused together, they may lack generative potential. They can become like a cast, woven around and around our broken bone and firmly held into place with adhesive. Once that bone is set back into place, the cast is no longer needed because only freedom of movement will promote growth and healing.

Similarly, we may lock our layers of labels and probabilities into place, prohibiting our own well-being. As we get to know our layers — their position, purpose, and their contribution to creating opportunity in our lives — we can loosen them, rearrange them, or even let them go so that our minds and hearts can become stronger, more agile, and increasingly resilient. This promotes additional possibilities for our future.

In addition to shifting position, we can reinterpret the meaning and purpose of each of those layers and their collective impact in our lives. Self-examination and self-discovery are continuous processes that reveal heightened and expanded possibilities for understanding, valuing, and appreciating who we are and what we can contribute to the world.

Our identity is also open to reinterpretation. The meanings we associate with our identity can and should change, and do so frequently; this is an important part of learning, maturation, and transformation. We do not need to accept other people's stories about who we are or ought to be; nor do we have the right to create limiting stories about other people.

There are also many, many possible interpretations of our mental illness and its potential impact in our lives. We too often choose the one that is the most disempowering, limiting, and devastating. This is a very important personal choice, and we have a responsibility to ourselves and to others to discover and project an understanding of mental illness that reflects the most alluring possibilities, such as perpetual renewal, appreciation of individuality, harmonious vibes, and peaceful coexistence.

While a student at that Catholic college, I learned about the concept of absolutism. According to this philosophical approach, there are certain laws about religion, politics, ethics, and other aspects of the world that are always true regardless of the situation. Hurting another human being is wrong. The earth is round. There are 16 ounces in a pound. Principles such as these are commonly accepted and for the most part unquestioned. They aren't just probabilities; they are certainties. For the true absolutist, there is no grey area.

You might have guessed that I am not an absolutist. I believe that yes, a multitude of things are commonly understood to be the truth, but in most cases there is and should be room for interpretation. While certainties may work well for calculating financial projections and probabilities are useful for gardening projects, neither is particularly helpful when it comes to the process of understanding our hearts and minds so that we can live a full and healthy life. Not only do certainties and probabilities lead to disappointment when they are used to meticulously map out our lives, they distract us from the immeasurably beautiful possibilities that we would not be able to imagine and fully experience if we relied solely on these predictive strategies.

Emphasizing possibilities shifts our focus away from setting expectations so that we can more fully explore our hopes and dreams. Living according to certainties and probabilities emphasizes the result or outcome of our behavior. Rather than measure our lives by arrival at a predetermined destination or how much we have accomplished, we can instead understand that our potential is dynamic and unpredictable but infinitely unique and beautiful regardless of the outcome.

Applying material laws to complex emotions is necessary to make a diagnosis. And a diagnosis can be a first step toward treatment that can help us function, fulfill cursory responsibilities, and feel more closely in alignment with our true selves. But a diagnosis is not the answer; rather, it ought to be the precursor to multiple questions that open up possibilities for deeper understanding and fulfillment. Rather than change and constrict who we are, this process helps us to actively construct our lives on an ongoing basis in response to what we experience, feel, and desire. A mental health diagnosis is not the destination, but a milestone on the journey of pursuing our purpose.

We are the curators of our lives. As we encounter thoughts, feelings, ideas, situations, and things, we can intentionally choose to include those that will contribute the most beauty, intrigue, and happiness. And those that would spoil our otherwise lovely lives can be set aside. We can arrange the gallery of our thoughts and feelings, highlighting those that are valuable to us so that we benefit from repeated exposure to them. The gallery can be rearranged as needed so that it is refreshed and reflects our current beliefs and needs.

We are also cultivators and creators. Botanical curators prepare soil, plant seeds, and tend to plants so that they produce a bountiful yield. We can positively influence the conditions of our lives, invite loving thoughts and nurturing feelings into our emo-cognitive ecosystems, and provide those thoughts and feelings with nourishment so that they may flourish.

Many, many years ago, I taught Saturday morning workshops about a variety of topics for people who were involved in community-based organizations. One student and respected colleague called me the "nonprofit guru" to demonstrate her respect for my knowledge and as well as my capacity to share that knowledge with others. Not quite so long ago, I started a blog called the "Activist's Muse." These two concepts illustrate the evolution in my life from know-it-all, wannabe expert to vulnerable lifelong learner. When we think we know everything, our curiosity is diminished. When we acknowledge that we don't know very much at all, lots of possibilities emerge. Wondering about what we don't know, including those things that we couldn't possibly ever know, stokes the fires of our creativity. The aim of learning becomes provocation and opening up our minds and hearts rather than performing a data dump of second hand knowledge.

Possibility is a special, lovely thing. It is an unlimited well of potential through which we can discover peace and fulfillment. By releasing the uninspired limitations of probability, we can glow with the possibility of our ideals and realize our dreams. Our mental illness can become a part of the possibilities for our lives rather than the primary probability.

Chapter Five
Perception Re-conception #3:
From Isolation to Integration

People can be understood either as a composite of discrete components or as a unified whole. When we understand ourselves to be a composite, we see ourselves as a quilted mishmash of many distinct but connected parts — for instance, the labels and identities that we have assumed. We experience mental illness and we like dancing, but they really don't have anything to do with each other. When we view ourselves as a unified whole, we see ourselves as an elaborate, fluid system of interrelated and interconnected pulses that continuously communicate and transform both individually and collectively. We experience mental illness and we like dancing, and when we dance we embody the varied and complicated emotions associated with our mental illness, and this reflects how both phenomena are rooted in our desire to feel more and more alive every day.

Our internal fragmentation can be exhibited and experienced in numerous ways. This may lead us to feel frustrated, angry, alone, phony, or sad. A similar type of disconnection can also exist between our inner and outer worlds, provoking feelings of anxiety, shame, or fear. Either way, parts of ourselves remain isolated from the greater whole when there is a lack of connection.

Our busy, complicated lives often result in competing priorities and divided loyalties. This relates to the various roles that we have assumed. We all have many roles that rotate throughout the day related to our family, profession, social circles, volunteer commitments, and personal interests. Each of our roles come with responsibilities, a system of accountability, expectations, and assumptions about our capabilities, will, and values. Our roles do not fully represent who we are as a person; they are an assemblage of what we anticipate doing in relationship to the needs and desires of other people in specific situations. Fulfilling our roles contributes to our personal satisfaction as well; they provide us with an opportunity to make a contribution, refine and master our skills, and achieve a particular result.

To keep things neat and tidy, we often see our roles as distinct and unrelated. We keep our roles separate as much as we possibly can to minimize conflict. This is particularly encouraged by some workplaces where, for instance, a role as a mother might be seen as not only unrelated to the work performed but also unwelcome (note: please don't work in a place like that!). We may find ourselves behaving very differently according to the role that we are playing. Being able to adapt ourselves to our roles in this way helps us to successfully fulfill our obligations and feel confident in the fluency of our abilities.

Managing all of our roles can be a challenge, particularly when we have taken on too many roles relative to our available time or when some of our roles, and their underlying values and assumptions, are misaligned or in conflict with each other or with our core beliefs. While roles present us with an opportunity to enact our purpose, they can also detract from that purpose by diverting our attention away from our needs and desires. We may also think or behave in ways outside of our character when fulfilling a role. If this contributes to our ability to learn and expand our perceptions, then it is probably a welcome novelty. If it makes us feel sick inside, or like we need to pretend to be someone else for a chunk of time on a regular basis, then it is most likely not a helpful role for us to be playing.

The roles we play in our lives should present us with an opportunity to express our values and realize our potential, not to lose ourselves. Taken together, the various roles we play can present to the world, in various contexts, situations, and settings, our unique ideas and vision.

There is little room for mental illness in most of the roles that we play. It is sometimes mentioned as an adjunct to a role, such as "soccer mom with generalized anxiety disorder," but more likely it is not explicitly present in the presentation and fulfillment of our role-related responsibilities. Yet, somehow that part of us cannot remain separate and hidden. It is a part of who we are, and as such our mental illness influences the way we interpret and enact each of our roles — similar to the way our personality, character, experiences, and values shape the roles we play. Intellectually, we put mental illness in a box as we do with our currently unused roles so that it does not get in the way or create confusion. We are attempting to put mental illness away and pretending that it does not exist or lacks relevance, when really it is always there having an influence to some degree. By doing this — compartmentalizing various components of ourselves — we are promoting the stigma that prevents too many people who suffer because of mental illness from getting the help that they need.

Like the roles in our lives, time is also viewed in a fragmented way. We break time down into discrete moments, days, months, years, and decades. The present serves as the dividing line between the past and the future. We think about who we are now, who we used to be, and who we hope to become. Our life stories, histories, and future plans include specific cut-off points such as before X, after Y, and when Z. I sometimes see my own life in two parts — before I experienced a major trauma and after. We divide time into various sections of convenience rather than recognizing it as a continuous flow of energy — an ongoing process with indefinable parameters. Infinite potential can be found within every moment.

The world and our mind aren't truly fragmented in this way — it is our perceptions of them that are actually fragmented. We interpret time, our roles, and many other things as discrete and detached because it helps us to understand, describe, explain, and mobilize them. While we can't change time, and we have limited control over many of our roles, we can change our perceptions of these phenomena to reflect an understanding of their truly integrated and dynamic nature.

Within us, there are many interrelated components. These include our roles, feelings, perceptions, values, beliefs, and thoughts. With so many different aspects of who we are, things can easily get out of alignment. For example, our thoughts may not reflect our values or our beliefs may be jeopardized by a role we are expected to play. By being in touch with our values and purpose, carefully and comprehensively examining how these components intersect with each other and identifying disconnections and misalignments, we can work toward unification and integration. All of these aspects of who we are naturally influence each other and should effortlessly work together toward the exploration of our life purpose as well as its fulfillment.

Everything inside of us is interconnected, but we are also connected to everyone and everything that surrounds us. All living things share the air that we breathe. Every pebble, every drop of water, every person is unique and purposeful on its own and as part of a community. We are all part of a delicately balanced ecosystem. Its response to every anomaly echoes with consequences that reach far beyond the source. Humanity shares the earth and its resources, but we are also intimately connected through our values and desires — which are all too often compartmentalized rather than integrated into a larger and more inclusive whole. When we hurt another, we hurt ourselves. Everything we think, do, or say has an impact in the world, and we are transformed through the thoughts, actions, and words of others.

Mental illness can be summarized as a lack of connection. It emerges and flourishes when our mental or emotional networks have unnoticed or irreconcilable gaps, when we fail to recognize our connections to other people and to the planet, and when we feel a desperate sense of isolation from either our authentic self or from the outer world. Experiencing bipolar disorder is like living in a fragmented world that is both individually and socially constructed to be composed of conflicting opposites. The essence of my existence has been a journey toward reconciliation and inner peace.

We can harmonize our inner and outer worlds, resolving these disconnections and creating an extensive and responsive web of connections. This begins by recognizing connections between ourselves and others in simple, everyday ways. As you move through the day, notice how everyone and everything you encounter influences your thoughts and feelings. It might be very silly and superficial, such as "wow, I love those purple tights!;" but you may also notice a strong sense of empathy, compassion, or even repulsion. When you watch the news, appreciate how events half way around the world may have been influenced, even to a very small degree, by something you did or by your lack of action. Think about how you take everything in, and how that influences both the way you see the world and how you interact with and within it.

Feeling deeply connected to other people and living things promotes a sense of awe and wonder about our lives and the world. It provides us with the resonance needed to express kindness and compassion toward others and toward ourselves. Connection opens up more deeply nuanced emotions and enhances our capacity to explore and understand those emotions.

66

Along with recognizing the connections in our lives, we can express appreciation for the good fortune of our continued existence and our ability to nurture new and more resilient connections. Gratitude amplifies the transformative power of everything that we do, and strengthens our sense of connection as we work toward feeling fully integrated both internally and externally.

We can also promote integration by protecting and replenishing the Earth that has given so much to us. When we truly recognize the gifts that the Earth has shared with us throughout our lives, enriching our every moment on the planet, we will feel compelled to give back by protecting these precious resources from the devastating impact of abuse and by caring for the air, soil, and water as if they were the children of all people and animals who share this space and depend on it for continued survival.

As the world around us revolves, and the people and places that surround us transform in both affirmative and destructive ways, it can be difficult to maintain a sense of congruence and an appreciation for the many connections that link us to others. We may also be challenged to maintain the equilibrium of our internal integration as we get stuck in a specific mental or emotional space to protect ourselves or to make progress toward a specific goal.

Imagine you are driving on a long, winding road in a far away place. You are relying upon your GPS to lead you in the right direction. All of a sudden the GPS says in that know-it-all voice, "lost connection." Panic ensues. Without that connection to an unlimited supply of maps, you might never find your way back. You try to call for help, but your cell phone has zero bars and is totally useless. You are all alone and dependent on others for help, yet you are unable to communicate with anyone beyond the vultures that are circling just a few feet ahead.

This is what happens inside of us when we lose touch with our connection to ourselves, to other people and creatures, and to nature. We become dependent rather than engaged in reciprocal relationships, full of fear when things don't go our way, and we might even feel like giving up. It is very difficult to make responsible decisions, and those that reflect our purpose, given these conditions.

We can take proactive steps to ground ourselves in a way that provides ease of access to a sense of connection regardless of our life circumstances — even when we are literally lost. When we are frustrated, fearful, or have the blues, we can tap into this connection to open ourselves back up to the possibilities of living in harmony with ourselves and with others.

Repeated exposure and continual engagement build fluency. This is true for learning a language, mastering a new skill, expanding our perceptions, and strengthening our connections. Fluency is not just the ability to recite information in a correct and comprehensive manner, it means that we have developed the capacity to use what we have learned in resilient and creative ways. When we develop fluency in a language, we are not only to write and speak that language by the book; we can use that language to communicate ideas and feelings beyond the words we choose to represent them. Similarly, when we develop fluency in our ability to feel connected, we will continue to discover increasingly intricate webs of connection within and all around us.

This fluency can be developed by nurturing our connection to our selves, to other people, and to the planet. To nurture our internal connection, we can identify our core values, purpose, and ideals and draw them near by providing them with opportunities to emerge as we go about our lives. We can evaluate how we have unintentionally excluded or intentionally included them, and veer toward the latter as often as possible going forward. Meditation can help us to silence things like the voices in our heads, those resident storytellers who will hijack our happiness if we don't exert some influence over the script, and external noise that can drown out the song in our hearts if left unchecked. By meditating, we can go inward, experience our presenting feelings, notice our thoughts without examination and rumination, and discover a pristine still space where all of our most precious resources are flourishing and patiently waiting for us to engage and integrate them. Like food, water, and air, we consistently need these resources — our dreams and values — to live a full and meaningful life.

When we feel internally connected, it is easier to connect with others. We see in others what we have the capacity to see in ourselves, and they reflect back to us the beauty, mystery, and tragedy of the human experience. We can develop connections with others by being our authentic selves, expressing empathy, and sharing our time and resources. Granted, sometimes other people will feel threatened and negatively react when we are authentic because they have not yet developed their own capacity to appreciate this depth of sincerity. In these cases, we should — and I know it can be somewhere between difficult and almost impossible — be compassionate and hope that they too will learn the many joys of being lovingly honest. It can be hard to cope when we suffer the rejection of other people. We must remember that they are rejecting the part of themselves that we have helped them to more clearly see, and that there are many other people who would welcome our presence. We can build connection, even with those who do not understand us, by listening to better understand who they are and what they desire. This may strengthen our connection to our own values, or expand our perception of what those values could possibly be.

Immersion in nature strengthens our connections not only to the planet but also to ourselves and to all other living creatures. Even if you aren't a tree hugging, dirt-digging hippie, you can enjoy nature in simple ways by listening to the birds sing, observing the leaves as they change colors in the fall, watching the shifting cloud patterns as a storm approaches, preparing fresh, local foods, and feeling the sun's rays on a warm summer day. Visiting natural places like the beach, the woods, a park, or a working farm can also restore our connection to the Earth. You can buy a plant for your home (bamboo is calming and usually thrives when cared for by those of us who lack green thumbs); bringing nature into your living space in this way creates a manageable indoor-outdoor integration that purifies the air and provides opportunities to connect with nature even when we are somewhat isolated from it by four walls and a roof.

Our insecurities are rooted in a loss of our center, purpose, and focus. They are exacerbated by feelings of disconnection from other people and the planet. When we lack inner connection and feel insecure, we may seek anchors to ground ourselves in other people, material objects, or drugs. These anchors weigh us down; they represent dependencies that deplete us rather than reciprocal relationships that are uplifting. As we discover and create new connections, we need to be careful that they do not become distorted in this way. Connections to others and to nature should be balanced, nurturing, and affirmative while promoting our emotional growth.

We sometimes seek completion of ourselves in other people and in things, rather than to complement them as part of a larger whole. When we view ourselves as incomplete, we are left with sore, raging gaps along with the need to fill in those gaps to minimize the pain of this isolation. It is unfair to use people and objects in this way (who wants to be plugged into a sore, raging gap?). When we think of ourselves as whole, we are ready to engage with the world in a complementary way — adding value and beauty to everything around us. This is what it means to live with integrity.

We can promote integrity by being intentional. An intention is a deeply rooted desire that is thoughtfully expressed through our words and actions. It is a sincere and authentic representation of who we are that also recognizes the potential impact we might have on others and the planet. When we act with intention, we infuse our actions with purpose. We take great care to think, do, and say things that reflect our virtue and add value to the world. Being intentional not only minimizes harm to ourselves and to others, it improves our sense of control and attitude, resulting in the creation of more favorable conditions.

We cannot fully understand our mental illness in isolation from the greater whole of who we are, including components such as our identities, personality, aspirations, and beliefs. Nor can we fully understand mental illness — our experience as well as that of others — without also taking into account the context of our relationships and environment. Understanding is fundamental to the process of healing and becoming whole. It feeds our ability to connect inward and outward. Understanding and connection are processes that build upon each other, resulting in more complex networks of ideas, feelings, and relationships.

All of us are fragmented to some extent. Our roles and identities create fractures in our lives. We are made up of the part of us that is mentally ill and the part that knows we can be healthy. We sometimes think in black and white, forsaking the full rainbow of possibilities within and around us. We isolate ideas, feelings, and activities because it simplifies our lives. Despite these divisions, we can continually promote holistic integrity and harmonious unity by creating, nurturing, and strengthening our connections.

Chapter Six
Perception Re-conception #4:
From Immobility to Fluidity

Mental health diagnoses represent a specific pattern of thoughts, feelings, and behaviors over a period of time. When we exhibit these characteristics, and it has been objectively confirmed by a professional with mental health expertise, we can assume that our thoughts, feelings, and behaviors are, in fact, representative of a particular mental health condition. While diagnoses represent these dynamic patterns, we sometimes think of our diagnosis as a state of being or as an identity. When this is the case, our diagnosis can become entrenched in our self-concept, and thus difficult to transcend. We become stuck and unable to move through our diagnosis to live a more whole, happy, and healthy life filled with purpose.

We can also become stuck as the result of traumatic live experiences. I experienced a great trauma on what was to be my first day of high school. There have been times, when my mind was clear of the everyday minutiae that often fill our heads up with junk, that I have woken up in the morning thinking it was time to get ready for school on what should have been a very special day. I also spent years after this traumatic event trying to live up to the hopes and dreams I had for my life at that time. I not only failed at this endeavor; I felt unfulfilled in the process of trying. I finally realized that the hopes and dreams I had for my life at 14 years old no longer represented the totality of my life aspirations. I also spent a lot of time wondering what my life might have been like at various stages if I had not experienced this trauma. I was retreating into the memory of who I once was and who I could have become, rather than growing into the person I was becoming.

We can feel trapped or stuck because of labels, circumstances, and life events; this entrapment can lead to complacency and apathy. Complacency and apathy reflect a lack of trust that the future will be filled with happiness and joy as well as a detachment from our personal ability to create a better future. They occur when we feel we are no longer in control of our lives. Unlike contentment, when we feel a sense of peace and harmony with the choices we have made, complacency results in us neglecting to make both everyday and important life choices that impact both our selves and the world around us. We give up, and resign ourselves to whatever happens to happen. Apathy is a more severe detachment that occurs when we stop caring about people, places, and things. It represents a lack of empathy and can lead to making choices, or intentionally failing to make choices, which result in pain and suffering.

We feel apathetic and complacent when we have become disenchanted with life. Disappointment after disappointment can lead us to believe that we are destined for failure and unhappiness. We can become programmed to expect a continuation of the painful and scary aspects of our most challenging life experiences, and when this happens the beautiful mysteries of life that might lead us to creatively wonder and dream are distorted and overshadowed.

Continued feelings of complacency and apathy may lead to a sense of hopelessness and desperation, further clouding our judgment. We can get stuck in destructive patterns of thinking and acting without even realizing we are doing so. Because we lack awareness, we also do not recognize that we may have other options that would more fully engage our thoughts, feelings, and aspirations — potentially leading to different and more favorable results. When we act out of desperation, we might conversely think that we are doing what is for the best given the circumstances. And we may be right; there are times when our options are severely limited given the context of the current situation, and we need to make what would otherwise be considered poor choices in order to survive. But when we consistently act in this manner, enacting deep feelings of desperation because we have given up on all or a part of our lives, it becomes more and more difficult to restore a sense of hope, dignity, and self-respect. Our challenges escalate and accumulate, building thicker and deeper walls that keep us in an undesirable place while also making it more and more difficult to both see that there are other options and to move toward those opportunities.

We also think and act in desperate ways when we become attached to a particular status or outcome so fervently that we would do nearly anything to maintain something that has given our life meaning or to achieve a related goal. Similarly, we sometimes act out of desperation when we are struck with the reality that life is turning out different from our expectations. When we are attached to our thoughts, ideas, beliefs, and life goals, alternatives — whether real or imagined — can jeopardize our identity and sense of security, resulting in a reaction that exacerbates the division between our self-concept and the enactment of that ideation. .

We can also find ourselves overwhelmed by hopelessness and stuck in its grip in less arduous ways. Hopelessness becomes normalized when we become too comfortable in what is truly an uncomfortable situation. These situations may include a job that bores you to tears, a marriage that has lost its passion, and a house that doesn't feel like a home. Staying in these situations without exploring other possibilities can lead to boredom, resentment, and, later on, regret. We can instead start moving toward other possibilities, such as building on what we already have in place so that it more fully reflects our needs and desires or working towards creating a totally new life situation. When large leaps are not feasible, taking small steps can strengthen our sense of choice and control and restore our optimism, while also improving our quality of life in the interim. It may not be practical or even desirable to move to a new location, but you can spring clean, create more open space, repaint, invite friends to visit, or redecorate to make your home an oasis of comfort and a peaceful sanctuary. I won't provide you with suggestions for infusing your marriage with more passion; that is, I'm afraid, a topic for an entirely different book — and one that I am sadly unqualified to write.

Immobilization can also be caused by congestion. Congestion is a cloudiness that engulfs us when we are physically, mentally, or emotionally backed up or overwhelmed. This lack of clarity can impede our ability to completely assess our options and to move forward; it is a smothering smog that both blocks our vision and our ability to take action. Congestion can develop under a variety of circumstances, such as: being super busy and pulled in competing directions; accumulation of useless objects or harmful, repeated thoughts; lack of physical activity; or flooded emotions.

If you have ever been to an area where there is a large pool of stagnant water, you know how awful it can be. A slimy film grows on the top, it smells yucky, and mosquitoes fly about ready to bite the first sucker who walks past them. When we become congested — when we lack movement and regeneration — we similarly lose our ability to experience pristine clarity in our thoughts and feelings because we have become saturated with the slime of stagnation.

Bodies of water have sediment, including pebbles, soil, and debris, that settles at the bottom. When there is a storm, that sediment can get disturbed and become mixed in with the water. At the same time, new elements are introduced which later become sediment once the rains have settled. When the skies are still, the water is clear as the sediment is neatly settled in the water bed. In our lives, there are memories and feelings that we let settle to the bottom. We let them go so that we can see more clearly. This sentimental sediment remains in our life and a part of us, but it no longer clouds our vision or interferes with our flow. When storms come our way and old stuff gets stirred up, our minds can become muddied once again. In these cycles of stormy and calm times in our lives, we can decide whether to let our feelings, thoughts, and beliefs remain a part of us, settle deep down for future use, or pass through us and move further downstream.

Challenging life experiences can activate things that we have let go — sometimes in unexpected or terrifying ways. For example, the death of someone close to us can bring up feelings associated with past experiences of loss and bittersweet memories of our time with those loved ones. While it may be difficult to process these emotions, especially at first, the alternative would be to block out those related memories and an important part of who we are. When we allow ourselves to experience the complexity of our feelings, and make connections among our past and present emotions, we can move toward greater self-understanding and compassion.

There are times that we may decide to intentionally let something go for good because it is not serving us well. For example, we might want to release interpretations of experiences that keep us stuck mentally and emotionally. We can release these feelings and beliefs, allowing them to decay and disintegrate. Decaying creates space for rebirth and opportunities for continual renewal. By letting go, we can promote movement in our emotional growth. Life is a delicately balanced process of continually decaying and becoming more alive.

Our habits can also become tinged by immobilization, stagnation, and congestion. We can get stuck doing or thinking about things in a particular way because of ease and convenience, regardless of their utility and capacity to add joy our lives. Examining our habits and either changing them or intentionally recommitting to them can help us to ensure that we are acting with clarity and moving in alignment with our life purpose.

If we feel stuck and decide to make a change in our lives, we might get started by exploring and pushing beyond the boundaries that we have constructed. As we begin, we may start and stop — or take these steps in scattered or unhealthy ways. We may also have fleeting thoughts that take us in multiple directions, leading us nowhere in particular. When the process of getting unstuck is grounded in the wellspring of our values and aspirations, we can more freely move in the direction of our conscious choice. As we dislodge all of the ideas, thoughts, feelings, habits, and circumstances that have held us hostage, we can make sense of everything we encounter and evaluate how to proceed within this context. This is easier said than done, of course, but becoming more and more aware and remembering to connect deep within ourselves is a good first step.

Change is scary to many people, and scary may be an understatement in some cases! Even when there is a tenable positive outcome, change brings with it many unknowns and can challenge our ability to feel physically and emotionally secure. For example, a person who has a destructive habit would likely be healthier and live a more full life if that habit were released or replaced with a healthier habit; yet, the process of changing that repeated action also requires transformation in thoughts, feelings, and identity in order to be sustainable. Changing these manifestations of who we think we are at the moment can threaten our self-concept. The process of change can also be tedious, burdensome, and exhausting, further repelling us. Even though change can be exciting and yield lovely new possibilities for our lives, we sometimes resist it and go to great lengths to prevent changes from taking place. We might also make excuses to put our life on hold or to not pursue something that we truly feel is worthwhile. When we resist change because it is the easier thing to do, the resulting immobilization may prevent us from enjoying meaningful activities and achieving our life goals.

We have many intrinsic resources that can be tapped into and mobilized to help us start moving, to start exploring our options, and to start living the life we deserve. Choosing the right resources from moment to moment will help us to start moving and live through change in the ways that are right for us.

My brain has been trained to use anxiety as fuel. It burns out quickly and leaves a polluting residue. It needs to be continually replenished, so I repeatedly poison myself as I keep using this fuel. When I use anger as fuel, it gets burned up really quickly, tingeing my fingertips and depleting my energy, and if I'm not careful it can lead to a raging inferno. Love, on the other hand, is a luscious, replenishing, renewable resource. The more I use it, the more it self-generates both within me and around me. These are just a few examples of resources that we can use as we move from immobilization to fluidity; others may include wit, sensitivity, or optimism.

Much immobilization occurs because we make significant investments of energy in our past and the anticipated future while overlooking the potentiality of the present moment. We also tend to view time as a collection of sequential, discrete moments rather than as a dynamic flow of energy. In a college theology class, my professor told us that there were two views of time. According to him, the Western view has a specific beginning point and moves in one direction while the Eastern view of time is a circle that also moves in one direction but continually repeats itself. I proposed that time was instead a spiral, with no beginning and no ending, through which cycles build on those that have occurred in the past. The past and the future are present in us right now as we think and feel.

The past is so very important to who we are today. Our experiences and relationships have helped to shape our values, attitudes, character, and expectations for life. As we recall memories, they clarify our priorities and connect us both inward and outward. Our past predates our birth; ancestral experiences are imprinted in our hearts and in our epigenetic code. We are also influenced by the past experiences of others as we interact with them, as they have been influenced by those with whom they have interacted in the past.

The future, in our minds, is a creative play space for our dreams. It is a place where we can test our assumptions and enact our ideals. The future is full of hope and offers new opportunities to realize our potential. It is a time when we will be able to reconcile our failures and aspirations.

The past and future may hold other meanings for us. We develop narratives in our minds to examine what has happened in the past and to have language to share those stories with others. These stories may evolve over time, weaving in more complex understandings of our life experience. Or they may degrade to the point where we have an overly simplistic view of our past that we are unable or unwilling to change. We may anticipate and dread terrible things in the future, or think that we have no future at all. These, too, are narratives that we have developed to help us in our quest for self-understanding and to cope with our fears. Let's look at a few examples.

Earlier in the chapter, I mentioned that I experienced a great trauma many years ago. For a long time after this event, I had an end of my life, end of the world story that I told myself and the selected therapists whom I let in on my secret. This story kept me stuck in the past and made me feel even more powerless to live a full life of my own making. Today that narrative has changed, and I see this event as a life saving experience that derailed me when I was on a destructive hormone-infused manic path. I didn't deserve what happened to me, and there may have been other ways for me to be helped at the time, but this particular trauma in the long run strengthened my intuition, empathy, and sensitivity. It has made me a better person, and one who is very generous in helping others. That doesn't mean that I deserved what happened or that I am grateful for the experience, but I have chosen to reinterpret this experience in a more meaningful and transformative way. My narrative about mental illness has also changed, as I think you have already discovered from reading this book! And those narratives are continually evolving; I will continue to write and rewrite my life story as I learn more about myself, my needs, and my desires.

I recently was on a job interview and was asked, "what question did you prepare to answer that we didn't ask?" I gave an honest answer, which might explain why I did not receive a call back for a second interview. I explained to the committee that I typically do not prepare responses to interview questions because I prefer to answer spontaneously and engage in conversation with the interviewer(s); when I prepare for specific interview questions, I get nervous and trip over my words. When we overprepare for the future, we may fail to live up to our expectations and find ourselves so busy trying to execute the scripts we developed that we cannot fully experience and enjoy life as it is happening.

Time is a subjective phenomenon. I believe that transformation is a continuous process with no beginning and no end. Changing from one state to another isn't like flicking a light switch. Our status — sick, healthy, happy, sad —is a representation of who and how we are at one particular moment in time. We may cling to our status, either dearly or fearfully, but it always has the potential to change. Our identity can be fluidly reinterpreted to reveal new, more complex meanings. Every moment reveals expanded opportunities for learning and growth and unlimited potential for transformation.

The rhythm of our flow may adjust according to what is happening in our lives. We do not always change, or recognize a new status, at a fast pace. Dormant seasons are important for rest and reflection. They prepare us for a luminous and brilliant emergence. Nature offers many examples of this including flowers, trees, butterflies, and animals that hibernate. Like our friends in nature, we, too, need times to slow down and rejuvenate.

I'm slowly learning to let it all go and let life flow. Rather than constraining or containing my identity, thoughts, and feelings, I allow them to move freely so that I can gracefully flow through the cycles of my life with more ease and joy. I have developed presence; the ability to respond to spontaneous moments and feel fully alive from moment to moment. Things within me are always in motion, yet I feel a peaceful harmony inside. I know that my every thought and action has the potential to heal the world. I no longer feel trapped or stuck; I am free.

Chapter Seven
Perception Re-conception #5:
From Rigid to Responsive

Life can seem predictable at times. Regardless of our best intentions and concerted efforts to improve our lives, we may continue to encounter people, ideas, and circumstances that seem surprisingly similar to those that we have experienced, and rejected, in the past. This can be repetitive, monotonous, excruciatingly boring, and frustrating.

The world, and everything in it, is continually evolving. Yet, our perception of that world, and the internal scripts that we use to describe and understand everything that we encounter, can be repetitive. We may see the same patterns in our lives and all around us that we have always seen — regardless of evidence that could potentially inspire new imagined possibilities. When our ideas and perceptions are based on past experience, despite the dynamic nature of life, a continually increasing gap between the life we desire and what we observe in our daily lives emerges — resulting in increased feelings of disconnection, loneliness, and isolation.

Rigid beliefs and expectations dull our senses and prohibit our ability to fully experience life in the moment as it is lived. They promote conformity to our limited perceptions of the past, keeping us frozen in time, rather than creating space for happiness, learning, and transformation right now. Rigidity reflects immobility as well as a self-centered harshness that keeps us trapped in a small, desolate, reactive world.

When we are rigid and lack flexibility, we are unable to notice, understand, and adapt to the needs and desires of others. In fact, we subconsciously expect others to adapt to us whether or not this is our best interest, their best interest, or the best interest of humanity and the planet. Rigidity constructs arbitrary barriers that sever relationships and cut us off from the joy of vivid experience, further isolating us from the goodness that is all around and stifling the development of our human potential.

Our beliefs, feelings, and expectations shape and are shaped by our self-concept, relationships, and environment. We can experience rigidity in all of these areas — within ourselves, in other people, and in the unwritten rules of society. By thinking through some of the ways rigidity might appear in our lives, we can be more prepared to recognize and redirect this unbecoming behemoth of a perceptual limitation.

I have endured a lot of voluntary and involuntary social isolation throughout my life because of my beliefs and behaviors. While my eccentricity is sometimes misunderstood or looked down upon by others who have a very limited definition of 'normalcy,' I often find those narrow views to be objectionable and terrifying. I gravitate towards people who share my ideals and veer away from those that I do not understand. In my head and heart, there are artificial lines drawn to declare what I will and will not tolerate. I will happily tolerate, even enjoy, many things that most people find difficult while I turn up my nose at things that other people tend to think of as fun or interesting. My lines are likely very different from yours; because they are invisible, it takes some form of communication for us to negotiate whether or not our lines intersect or create an overlapping space.

But we sometimes draw those lines for ourselves and for each other without sufficient exploration and communication to determine their precise location. We too often fail to question why those lines were drawn in the first place, and whether or not their location accurately represents our interests and beliefs.

These lines are drawn not only by individuals but also by social groups. Groups implicitly or explicitly expect conformity within these lines in order for someone to remain a part of the group. If a member of the group steps over the line or attempts to erase it, she or he may jeopardize their position within the group and their continued membership.

Let's look at this book for an example. As I write and share my various ideas about mental illness as informed by my life experience and philosophy, I realize that I may offend the sensibilities of other people — people who experience mental illness, those who have dedicated their lives to helping us heal, and the people I interact with every day who have no clue that I have a diagnosis of bipolar disorder. Of course, this is not my intention; I am writing this book in an effort to be helpful and to create expanded opportunities for dialogue and activism related to mental health treatment. Sometimes we offend other people just by being ourselves, regardless of our intentions. And, in return, we may feel offended by others who are doing nothing more than just being themselves and trying to do something positive in the world.

These rigid lines are difficult enough to navigate on a one-to-one basis and within the social groups to which we belong. In reality, lines are coming at us from all directions — from multiple people, groups, organizations, and cultural messengers simultaneously. We take these surrounding lines to construct boundaries that define who we are, what we believe, what we will and won't do, and our goals in life. Boundaries are very useful when they protect us and others from harm. But when they are unexamined, inflexible, and confining, they stand between us and our ability to explore and to experience the sustained happiness that is generated through continued curiosity and adaptive learning.

We all have little shortcuts that we use to make generalizations and to make quick judgments. These shortcuts may save time and make life easier in certain circumstances. For example, if we decide that we do not like the color red, then we do not need to ever consider integrating anything of this color into our lives. We can skip over racks of red dresses at the clothing store. But these shortcuts are not always so benign. If we decide that we want to exclude certain feelings, types of people, or a range of experiences from our lives, then we may be limiting our transformative potential and we could also potentially cause harm to others. Evaluating people, things, or circumstances based on rigid guidelines, without any consideration for their uniqueness or their potential, stunts our intellectual and emotional growth.

We also evaluate and judge ourselves using arbitrary measurements. We may think we are too much of this and too little of that — too tall, too short, too thin, too plump, too poor, too rich, too depressed, too anxious, not happy enough. All of these terms are relative because their meaning is nebulous and varies from person to person and situation to situation; yet, when we use them in this way, they represent an objective gauge that can unfortunately be equivocated with our self-worth and prevent us from both loving ourselves and pursuing enjoyable activities.

In our busyness and steadfast dedication to recovery from mental illness, we can easily overlook or ignore the little lights of pleasure and passion that illuminate what can otherwise seem like a dark, dingy, and dismal world. These treasures are available to bring abundant enjoyment and happiness to our lives, but we may avoid them if they stir up memories of a manic mood, and its dire consequences that remain long after the mood has passed, or if they are inaccessible because we have lost hope and find them to be trivial reminders of our mundane existence.

Our expectations for what might happen in the future can also be rigid. When we anticipate specific events or times in the future, we might associate words such a wonderful, horrible, exciting, or embarrassing with what we expect to happen. We might also have fixed ideas about the way things will unfold or the outcome of this experience. These rigid expectations can result in disappointment and also make it difficult for us to be fully aware and actively respond to life with openness as it happens.

All of these examples demonstrate how rigid perceptions can limit our experiences and alter the course of our lives. When we judge rather than listen to cultivate understanding, and when we react rather than respond, our suffering is compounded. We both internalize and externally propagate coarseness, forsaking a transformative opportunity to both learn and to feel a deep, selfless, endless love.

Rigidity is rooted in negative emotions such as fear and anger. Negative emotions can either energize and motivate us or shut us off and break us down. When the latter happens, rigid reactions to life filter and distort our experience — leading to a deepening unhappiness that seems to have no end. Instead, we can use these emotions, such as fear and anger, to become more responsive. Fear can help us to notice anomalies in feelings or our surroundings. When we feel a burst of fear because something in awry, we can choose to be invigorated by this alarm to become more alert and aware of what is happening. While anger may feel unpleasant, it also severs open the raw, delicate spaces in our hearts that might otherwise remain hidden. By recognizing and tapping into this empathic resource, our ability to respond, rather than react, is strengthened.

I have a lot of definite ideas about the world. I strongly believe that people should always be kind to themselves and to one another, that animals deserve our love and reverence, and that all people are entitled by birth to equitable opportunities. While these ideas are very important to me, they are not shared by all people; in fact, some people might find these ideas ridiculous or offensive. They have been shaped by my life experience, values, and personality and, since my experiences, values, and personality are unique to me, I can't expect that all other people will universally share my views. And when people do share my views, it wouldn't be fair for me to assume that they hold these beliefs for the same reasons as me.

These and other ideas that I have about the world influence the way I interpret my personal experiences and act as a guide for my choices. They serve an important purpose in my life. They make me who I am, and who I aspire to become. But they can also limit my relationships with myself and with others if I allow them to become objective truths that do not allow any space for exploration of alternatives.

I have three cats at home, and I adore them. They are spoiled silly. Not everyone shares my love of cats, or of animals in general. I do not eat animals, but many people who have pets that they love do eat meat. This is difficult for me to understand, because I have made a different choice in my life based on my very strong values. I could choose to rigidly respond to these pet loving meat eaters by excluding them from my life, berating them in front of our peers, or throwing red paint on their doorstep. But these rigid reactions would cause emotional harm to others or physical harm to their property. They would not be an expression of my values, nor would they promote the dialogue and exploration necessary for others to potentially expand or shift their views.

When we attempt to influence others, we too often defensively interrogate opposing points of view rather than seek mutual understanding through open-minded, compassionate conversation. Mental health treatment has often felt one-sided to me in this way. We can choose to respond to each other — to listen, share, and empathize — instead of reacting in hurtful ways that result in everyone involved retreating into the safety of their shrinking preconceptions. When we respond to each other rather than react, we become less resistant and more resilient.

When we call the police, fire department, or ambulance in an emergency, we expect someone to arrive on the scene as soon as possible. One time, about 25 years ago, I called the police because I thought someone was trying to break into the house. They did not get there until more than an hour later. Luckily, I was still alive when they got there, but I shall forever be emotionally scarred by the memories of huddling in a corner on the floor waiting to die at the hands of a merciless stranger.

When our feathers are ruffled because something is said or done that challenges our values, we sometimes react as if it were an emergency. We take immediate action to resolve our differences without giving the situation or how it could be handled any serious thought. The consequences of our reaction also aren't fully considered; we can only think about our next move and how it will prove our point or improve our position.

In these circumstances, we can give ourselves permission to not react right away. We can slow down and allow ourselves adequate time to respond in accordance with our values and goals. When we feel compelled to react, we can instead pause to observe and fully experience the emotions associated with those reactions so that we can make informed decisions. We can take time to think things through and carefully evaluate our options.

As we become more aware of the complexity of our feelings, the source of our thoughts, the consequences of our actions, and the needs of other people and the planet, we become more tuned in to our intuition. Intuition is a wise inner guide that both protects us from danger and steers us toward experiences that add value, joy, and beauty to our lives. It emerges through an integrated connection of our values, purpose, and desires. As our connection to intuition is developed and becomes more readily available to us, we can trust in this resource to help us respond to other people and the world in which we live in loving, life-affirming ways.

Being responsive means that we are purposeful in all of our actions and interactions. We consistently live in congruence with our most precious values, and both refine and strengthen our commitment to those values through their enactment.

There may be times that require us to affirm our values by steadfastly, even stubbornly, holding our position. When we experience or observe injustice, for example, our intuitive response may be to illuminate inequities and work toward their resolution. Responding to others and to situations that conflict with our values means that we listen, seek understanding, and promote peace and harmonious coexistence. Rigid reactions result in more unresolved conflict. If those injustices are dire and people, animals, or the planet are not safe, then responding from our heart — with a little help from our head — can help us to develop a strategic and sustainable solution in partnership with our allies.

Responding softens our approach to self-understanding and interaction with others. It offers us flexibility and the opportunity to create the sort of life that reflects our deepest individual and collective desires. Responsiveness provides us with the time needed to cultivate understanding so that we do not need to rely on hard and fast rules that may no longer be relevant or helpful when important decisions need to be made.

Being responsive requires openness. We need to be open to possibilities, to diversity of thought, and to continual evolution and change in order to respond in our life. We also need to be trusting, both in ourselves and in others, to discover the courage needed to respond rather than react with rigidity. When we are open and responsive to the needs of others, we must first honor our own needs and desires before we can effectively appreciate and understand how others are feeling and thinking.

Several years ago while at a spiritual retreat center, I crossed paths with a renowned Buddhist teacher for whom I once volunteered as a door guard at another event. As I walked by, I heard him jokingly say, "I hate you" to the colleague walking by his side. It took me by surprise, as it was not necessarily something I would expect someone who is committed to nonviolence to say. But I was not offended, nor was I shocked. In fact, I was amused. I felt grateful that he was just as snarky and silly as me.

Without even trying, he taught me a great lesson about responsiveness. If I had thought about his statement only in relationship to his vocation, I would probably have had a negative reaction. If I had said the same thing and someone understood what I said only within the context of my mental illness, they, too might have reacted with judgment. It has happened to me; my words have been grossly misinterpreted with very negative consequences only because I happen to have a diagnosis — not because I am witty and sometimes sarcastic. Unfortunately, some people treat people who have been diagnosed with a mental illness in unfair and cruel ways — like children or even worse. In turn, some of us with a diagnosis (myself included) can sometimes be too hasty in the interpretation of our experiences and the intentions of other people.

Approaching our relationships, and ourselves, with trust and openness allows us to exercise this discretion. We can expand our understanding and perceptions of the situation, rather than jump to hurtful conclusions with no opportunity for learning. This helps us to develop strong bonds with others, but bonds that are flexible enough to respond when these anomalies occur.

We can strengthen our ability to be responsive through regenerative activities that help us to discover and appreciate all of the beautiful, sacred spaces in our hearts. Getting sufficient rest brings clarity to our thoughts and synchronizes our inner rhythms. Taking care of ourselves through healthy habits keeps us mentally and emotionally agile. Immersing ourselves in beauty and creativity, such as by attending a free community concert or collecting colorful fall leaves, helps our inner light to glow and grow. All of these actions help us to restore our most cherished resources and create the time and space necessary for us to gently respond in all of our thoughts, actions, and interactions.

My story, and your story, is an ever-evolving mystery. As we actively and lovingly respond to life, bits and pieces of that mystery are revealed. Our dependence on rigidity diminishes as we develop and engage our curiosity through this process. Releasing rigidity allows us to move from giving and taking, where we control and manipulate others to get what we think we want, to co-creating a beautiful and purposeful life in harmony with other people and the planet.

Chapter Eight
Perception Re-conception #6:
From Austerity to Simplicity

If you have an interest in politics, perhaps you have heard the term "austerity budget." Austerity budgets are developed in difficult financial times, when resources are scarce, to control and minimize spending of either the government or of people in general. People sometimes develop an emotional austerity budget when our emotional wealth is viewed as a limited, finite resource that is in the process of being depleted. When this happens, we react to emotional drain and pain by blocking, withholding, and suppressing more and more of our emotions. We become cold, harsh, disengaged, and bitter. We lose hope.

Despite my unconventional views and creative approach to life, I grew up in a very austere Pennsylvania German (also known as Pennsilfaanisch Deitsch or "Pennsylvania Dutch") culture. The recent rash of Amish love stories and murder mysteries may lead those of you who have not been directly exposed to Pennsylvania German culture to believe it is one and the same with this Anabaptist religion. Many Pennsylvania German families actually are of non-Anabaptist denominations, such as Lutheran or UCC, and my family chose to be Jewish! But we do share other cultural commonalities such as food (although I'm a vegetarian), language (kannscht du micke fange?), and various folkways.

Since this culture has been a huge part of my life, and I have nothing but the utmost respect and love for my people, I can be honest about our weaknesses. Pennsylvania Germans are among the stingiest people around. We are cheap, cheap, cheap. We love telling stories about how poor our families are or used to be and how these experiences have added immeasurable value to our lives; they have made us stronger, more inventive, and more resourceful. We do without as a measure of our tenacity. We are also stingy with our compliments. We don't easily hand out kind words; in fact, one of my aunts had a dog named Ugly and a cat named Fatso. We value hard work and integrity and look down on those who fail to contribute in line with our expectations. The one area in which we typically express abundant generosity is food. Going to a family reunion is an hours-long smorgasbord of bread, cakes, pies, and more bread. It is a carb lovers' paradise. Our Anabaptist cousins probably think we are very "fancy," as they are even more austere than we are.

This mostly no frills existence is rooted in discipline, self-sacrifice, and denial of desires which are all considered to be acts of virtue. There are similar expressions of austerity in other cultures and subcultures. Perhaps this is why I was attracted to work in the nonprofit sector (aside from the very important fact that I wanted to devote my life to helping others) as I found within it familiar stories about hard work, sacrifice, and thrift. I have also seen patterns of women sacrificing their ambition and their values for the men in their lives — often without even realizing that they are doing it and the impact it has on their children and the world. There is also a lot of austerity in dieting; people who want to lose weight often deny themselves the pleasures of food rather than taking the time to enjoy the rich textures and vibrant flavors that nature has provided for our sophisticated, sensual palates.

My most beloved aunt once gave me a special sweet treat as a holiday gift. It was a combination of two of my favorite foods from one of my very favorite people. But ever conscious of my expanding waistline, I chose to share her thoughtful gift with my coworkers. I did not save even one bite for myself. My aunt passed away about a month later.

This act of austerity, of denying myself the enjoyment that she so wanted to me to experience, will haunt me forever.

More recently, I had a craving for strawberry shortcake. Strawberry shortcake is usually my birthday cake, and it is the only time I have it all year even though it is one of my favorite foods. After my family each has a slice of cake, I freeze the rest so that I can eat one slice at a time over the rest of the summer. But a few weeks ago, I couldn't resist my craving and I made a strawberry shortcake — in the middle of May — and I ate it every night straight for one week. A few weeks later, when strawberries were in season, I did it all over again. I have learned to indulge myself, but to do so responsibly.

I have also brought a great deal of austerity and asceticism into my work. Based on a strong sense of responsibility and a desire to make a difference, I have simultaneously worked multiple jobs, toiling away for long hours at the expense of a personal life. Because I work for the nonprofit sector to improve communities and to help people in need, and because those needs are so complex and so vast, it is difficult to stop. How can I ethically enjoy anything when so many people are suffering? After nearly 20 years of developing these work habits, I, too am suffering — much more so than I was when I first started all of those years ago. Work has become an addiction.

I have entangled myself in a web of commitments, work and otherwise. My strong sense of responsibility to those commitments compels me to get up and do something meaningful almost every day whether I feel like it or not. I am always engaged in purposeful work and contributing something that is of value to others. But at the same time, I feel that I have become somewhat lost because I have not adequately taken care of myself. I have sacrificed my own needs and desires for the common good. And while that isn't necessarily a bad thing, I feel the need to restore more balance to my life for the sake of my health and well-being. And despite the fact that I have felt this need for some time, I continue to overcommit to others. I make unrealistic promises, most of which I fulfill, leading me to feel that I am pulled in too many directions. This sometimes shifts the emphasis of my involvement from purpose and impact, where it ought to be, to busyness and productivity. While working hard is valuable and necessary for a full life, and my Pennsylvania Dutch ancestors would likely agree, it is not the beginning and end of all good things in life.

Some people are stingy in a different way; they withhold empathy and compassion from others. While I deny my own needs and desires for the benefit of the common good, many other people are unaware of, or do not care to understand, other people's feelings and dreams for their lives. They may also lack consideration for animals or for the planet. This lack of generosity in the hearts of others is yet another example of austerity and its harmful impact on individuals and our society. Sadly, I fear that this form of austerity is far more common than the type most intimately known to me.

Self-denial can manifest in many other ways. We may cut ourselves off from our feelings when they seem too overwhelming or reject good feelings for fear they will not last. We might think that we deserve to be hurt or to feel pain because it is all we have ever known or because we have been taught to dislike ourselves. We sometimes choose martyrdom over health and happiness. We expect and accept surviving when we could instead be thriving.

When austerity leads to the normalization of pain and suffering, beauty and joy can seem out of reach or even irrelevant and sometimes terrifying or disgusting. We might think that these lovely things are mere expressions of vanity or evidence of sloth. We may feel as though we are abandoning our cause — whether that cause is helping others through a community-based organization or helping the world understand the pain of our mental illness. A little austerity is useful if it helps us to develop humility and common sense. But too much austerity will aggravate and compound our emotional suffering.

I have become an expert at minimizing and avoiding pain. I know all of my triggers, and I go out of my way to steer clear of them. By doing this, I feel more comfortable and less threatened. I feel in control. But I also seal myself off from an awful lot of lovely life experiences.

Rather than evaluating the quality of life by the lack of pain I am experiencing, I could instead celebrate all of the love I have allowed myself to feel and that which I have shared with others. I could be grateful for the opportunity to live a life full of sustenance and substance rather than one of suppression and mere subsistence.

Austerity prevents us from fully experiencing and enjoying our lives. When we choose to be austere, or do so automatically without giving it much thought, we are denying not only our desires but also our self-worth. We position ourselves to be miserable. Instead, we can affirmatively choose to expand our capacity for happiness by creating openings for beauty, love, and peace to emerge. Austerity is a violent and toxic suffocation of all that is good; simplicity, on the other hand, is the result of purifying our minds and lives so that we are able to notice and appreciate even the smallest good fortune.

It has been difficult for me to discover ways to restore my natural purity because it has been so terribly tarnished and tainted by traumatic life experiences. In addition, modern culture seems to value mundane superficiality. My life experiences, and the sociocultural environment in which I live, have resulted in a lot of messiness and junk that complicate what could otherwise be a simple, happy life.

There are several things we can do to reduce mental, emotional, and physical waste — revealing a pristine simplicity that allows us to more clearly see and feel what truly matters in life. All of these types of waste are rooted in clinging to things we don't need because what we truly want seems scarce or unavailable to us. They result in clutter, confusion, and decay, preventing us from living a full, happy life. We can create more clarity and happiness by simply letting go and saying no.

Mental waste accumulates when we repeatedly make unhealthy choices and then justify or rationalize those choices based on bitterness or desperation. When we are inflexible in our thinking or harsh in our judgment of ourselves or others, more mental junk is added to the pile. These actions stifle us intellectually, preventing us from thinking about our life experiences and making decisions in new and creative ways.

Similarly, emotional waste builds up when our feelings are unexamined and unprocessed, and therefore continue regardless of their resonance with our values and ideals. When our feelings build up to the point that they overwhelm us, we are no longer able to fully engage with life. They control us, rather than guiding us as we navigate the twists and turns in our lives.

We might also surround ourselves with physical waste, or things that deplete our energy rather than add value to our lives. When we have more stuff than love in our lives, it becomes difficult to think and feel with clarity. There is a direct connection between our environment, including those things that we consider to be our personal possessions, and the way that we think and feel.

We often let things and ideas enter our lives out of convenience, or sometimes to be polite. It can be easier in the short term to just accept that this is the way things are than to question why things are happening or how they could be different or more favorable. But over time, taking in too much of the wrong things will unnecessarily complicate our lives. We can establish guidelines for what we want, based on our deepest desires rather than a depleting austerity, and then make choices that affirm who we truly are.

We should not deny ourselves the sweet indulgences that we deserve. Life is full of beautiful moments and opportunities to experience compassion for ourselves and others as well as joyful peace. When we live simply and eschew austerity, the reverberant energy of this beauty fortifies our vitality. Our capacity to feel awe, to wonder, and to explore our curiosity are expanded when we choose quality over quantity. Simple, natural indulgences, such as walking barefoot through a field of wildflowers, feeling the cool mist from a waterfall on a warm summer day, gazing at the stars on a crisp summer evening, listening to the laughter of children as they play, or eating a freshly picked apple, are restorative and make life worthwhile.

Austerity can exacerbate the symptoms of mental illness, and the personal and social insecurities that develop as a result of that illness can lead us to depend on austerity to function or to avoid destruction. By introducing simplicity to our lives — by removing junk and replacing it with awareness and appreciation — we can slowly begin to relax our reliance on the denial of our desires to create more space for happiness to emerge.

Chapter Nine
Perception Re-conception #7:
From Critique to Compassion

I come from a family of complainers. Nothing is ever good enough for us. We obsessively criticize our every flaw, as well as that of others. Very little escapes our intense scrutiny.

Critique can be the result of thoughtful analysis. It can help us to discern how people, things, and experiences align with our values and expectations, or don't. But when critique originates from fear or perfection, and when it results in unfair judgment, shame, jealousy, or avarice, it becomes a very unhealthy process that limits our ability to creatively change those things that we think could and should be better.

Throughout my life, I have found myself an unwilling target for other people's insecurities and anger. As a highly sensitive person, it was often too much for me to bear — provoking my own insecurities and anger, and even leaving me feeling suicidal at times. Their stories about who I was at the time and my value as a human being became interwoven with mine. I started to question my purpose and identity and, to some extent, believe the horrible things that were said about me or that I deserved the way I was treated. I had to choose to stop believing what was said to and about me and start believing in myself instead. I worked hard to re-write those co-written scripts so that they more accurately reflected my intrinsic and unadulterated thoughts, feelings, identity, and aspirations.

Self-victimization probably hurt me more than others could have possibly done on their own. I allowed their hostility to infiltrate my mind and destroy my ability to be happy. Thinking of myself as a victim, and later a survivor, was a source of strength. I was proud that I was able to overcome these obstacles and find happiness despite the challenges I experienced. Yet, I found myself too angry and stuck, and lacking in resilience, to be able to truly transcend these experiences, transform my life, and live as in a way that fully reflected who I was inside.

I have also been a terrible bully to myself. I constantly pick myself apart — my appearance, my work performance, my interactions with others, my life in general — and make lengthy lists of all of the things that I don't like about myself and mistakes that I have made (you may have noticed this a bit earlier in this book!). In addition, I have made mental notes about how I should change myself to better fit with others' distorted and one-sided view of who I ought to be. I hid those components of myself that violated this shallow image. This is a result of misguided trust in others; because others were unkind to me, I learned to be unkind to myself. I didn't carefully examine or contest their words and actions on a deeper level. I knew that what they were doing was morally wrong; yet, I absorbed much of what was said and done and instead questioned my own validity.

The kind of work I do is a paradise for critical people. People who choose to help others generally do so because they see what is wrong with the world and hopefully feel that they can be part of the solution. This means that people who have a tendency to be critical, like me, are drawn to the helping professions. It also means that the field is full of critical people, and you need to watch your every move.

I have also been compelled to help others professionally because I have a lot of personal experience with many of the same types of social, economic, and personal issues that have been difficult or even traumatic for people with whom I have worked with over the years. I've been there, and I have a deep understanding of the complexity of entrenched systems that influence and limit our personal choices and how we live our lives. I also understand how difficult it is to be more of who we truly are or aspire to be when so many things are not designed to work in our favor. Similarly, I have been embroiled in a battle between my social conscience and that which represents my unique individuality. There is an ongoing tension between personal and social spaces with each vying for power and control.

In response to the injustices I have observed and experienced, and my inability to cope and make sense of these experiences, I have repeatedly numbed myself in a number of ways. I have been dishonest about my desires, and even intentionally denied myself the joy of their pursuit and fulfillment. I have been caught in the trap of perfectionism where everything seems drastically unacceptable in relation to an unrealistic yet nebulous standard. Fear of failure has prevented me from taking action, and has led me to ruminate about every potential flaw for a long period of time before and after saying or doing something. I also worry about things that might happen in the future, even when their occurrence is highly unlikely. I have compared myself to other people, to their ideals, and to standards that don't really exist. I have also compared other people to my ideals and have judged them accordingly. I have felt envious of others, as well as sympathetic for their situation.

Being critical of myself and others is the result of the compounded shame and guilt I have accumulated over many trying years. All of these thoughts and actions have cheated both myself and the world of the many unique gifts that only I can create and share. They have sapped my energy for a noble cause, but one that has not helped me to generate sustainable change within myself or in the world. Criticism, and its cousin critique, have their place; but when used inappropriately or to excess they keep us stuck in the past and prevent us from envisioning a more vibrant future.

Rather than enumerate and ruminate about the things that cause me despair, I can do the same for those things that bring me joy and happiness. Every day, we can find something that evokes a sense of gratitude. They can be simple things, like the sun coming up in the morning, a day off from work, or a really good chocolate chip cookie. Or, they might be more personal, such as the ability to engage people in lively conversation (something I wish I had!) or a strong bond with another human being. If we look closely, there are so many things for which we can and ought to be grateful — even when there are so many terrible, awful, unbearable things that have happened and continue to happen in our own lives as well as in the lives of our fellow Earthmates.

We can experience more happiness and health, both emotional and physical, by shifting our focus from what is wrong to what is right. Putting our energy into good things gives them the support they need to grow and flourish. When we choose to see the good in other people, their ability to recognize and fortify those characteristics is expanded. This doesn't mean that we should overlook injustice or accept nastiness or sloppy performance. But when we give those things all of our energy, they remain in control and our ability, individually or collectively, to change them becomes diminished by their growing significance in our lives. It is not enough to identify and scrutinize the problem or deficit; we must also envision, develop, deeply believe in, and actively create a revolutionary resolution.

Happiness is not the absence of difficulty, but a lack of attachment to the difficulties that inevitably erupt in our lives. When we cling to all of the things we think are wrong, and this defines and guides our thoughts and behavior, we become trapped by the very things that we hope to avoid, abandon, or change. When we instead let these things go —

we notice and understand them but allow them to pass through us — they become malleable and transformable. We can change their underlying meaning in our lives and focus our attention on working toward something more desirable.

For example, I often experience irritability. Lately, that irritability has been exacerbated by a medical condition. If I define myself as irritable by saying, "I am irritable and it makes me feel like crap" it is being named as a part of my identity, the core of who I am, and therefore is difficult to change. If I am irritable and that's it, then there is nothing that reflects my aspirations. I could instead say, "I am feeling especially irritable at the moment, and I am grateful that this extreme feeling is making me more aware of my emotions." Or, I could say, "I am noticing thoughts in my mind that reflect irritable feelings; I am capable of generating additional thoughts that reflect my value and purpose." There are innumerable ways for us to go beyond the immediate critical thought to include those that are nurturing and fulfilling. Even if we sincerely believe these and similar follow-up statements, we must fully articulate our implicit assumptions as carefully and completely as we do our criticism. They deserve at least the same amount of attention, if not more.

To balance the criticism we generate and experience in our lives, we need to heighten our awareness of its presence and impact. We can sometimes be critical of ourselves and others as a matter of habit and not even realize that we are doing it. We replay internal scripts that pick apart both superficial and significant aspects of our lives. When we do this on autopilot, those scripts become more deeply internalized. Because we live in a world where there has always been a great deal of conflict and people openly express their dissatisfaction, often in hurtful and unhelpful ways, criticism is also entrenched in our environment. Noticing undue criticism that could instead be replaced or augmented with constructive, creative ideas helps us to retain our personal power and connect with our ability to make choices and positive changes.

We also need to be realistic and authentic. We can't expect ourselves to never think or express a critical thought. I know there are some lovely people who fit this description, and I admire them greatly, but most people are just not capable of sincerely never being critical. As I mentioned earlier, there are times when critique is necessary and useful. It can be helpful to define a goal or situation by what it is not, at least as a starting point. For example, if we have not yet fully developed a vision of what we would like our next profession to be, we can limit our choices to help clarify possibilities. There are certain things that I do not like to do or that I would find an ethical challenge; rather than criticize these occupations and the people who partake in them, I can instead choose to not let it be a part of my life. Authenticity allows us to be honest with ourselves about what we do and don't like or believe. But another part of being authentic is allowing our most pure, untainted by the harshness of our life experiences, nature guide us in our worldly interactions. We can elect to see the big picture, including both the "good" and the "bad," and not just what most suits our mood or our position at the time.

An abundantly generous heart helps us to see goodness in ourselves and others, even when that goodness has been hidden by trauma, lack of coping skills, or unruly personalities. The more we look for and discover this goodness, the more we and others will recognize its existence and significance. By being generous with our time and understanding, we can recognize and learn more about the complexity of most people and situations rather than judging them based on what we think we already know. We can open up opportunities to learn rather than creating blame and shame through our criticism. Generosity compels us to consistently share our best intentions with others regardless of our preconceptions.

Challenges are inevitable in our lives and in the world. There will always be differences of opinion and competing interests. We will have internal struggles that seem insurmountable. To be happy, we must accept that challenge is a part of life — and one that is integral to our emotional health. Challenges help us work through our thoughts and feelings, discovering new connections and novel approaches to engaging with difficult situations. They help us to discover our strength and cultivate resilience. Challenges force us to learn more about ourselves and about others, and create opportunities for personal and social transformation. When we accept that challenge, conflict, and criticism are going to happen whether we like it or not — and let go of the idea that we can expel or control these experiences — we will be better prepared to gracefully handle these situations and use them as tools for our personal development.

We must also accept other people as they are. This doesn't mean that we agree with harmful behavior, but that we recognize people at this particular step of their unique life journey rather than project our experiences, values, and aspirations onto them. Similarly, we can unconditionally love and accept ourselves by delighting in our imperfections, otherwise known as opportunities for learning and growth. When our heart overflows with generosity, we can provide the unconditional love and support that is needed to discover our current strengths while also imagining the vast untapped potential within each of us. If we don't love ourselves unconditionally, we can never truly be well. And if we don't love ourselves, we can't feel or express love to others.

Merely accepting ourselves or our situation is a great start, but feeling appreciative is even more transformative. We can appreciate our thoughts, feelings, experiences, resources, opportunities, and relationships by exploring their meaning to discover their unique value and contribution. By feeling and expressing appreciation, our generosity grows as does our ability to contextualize criticism by painting a bigger picture that includes all of the factors that reflect reality and influence our understanding.

Understanding takes into account all of the interconnected elements that together compose every person, organization, or situation. If I pass a random stranger walking down the street who says to me, "you're ugly," I might in response think, "you jerk" (or, if I'm honest, something a bit more severe). My response is a judgment; perhaps this individual is not a jerk but is a person who is suffering deep emotional pain and is crying out for help. Maybe this person has not had the privilege of a respectful conversation with another human being for a long time. This "jerk" might be experiencing a medical condition that results in odd behavior.

I often find myself being judgmental of other people. I see them through the lens of my own experience and capabilities. I sometimes think, 'if I can do it, why can't they?' This isn't fair, because other people are free to make their own choices. Others have strengths and capabilities that I don't have and might not even immediately recognize. They may also lack the ability or will to share those strengths with others. Understanding and appreciation means that we need to step outside of ourselves to clearly see people and things for what they are, and sometimes we need to set aside who we think we are or who we have become to discover our true, authentic nature and desires as well as those of others.

Our ability to complement criticism is also strengthened by being patient, kind, and forgiving of ourselves and of other people. When we forgive, we take into account everything that influenced a particular outcome. As we have additional experiences and take in new information, we continually calibrate and integrate our internal and external worlds. We grow in response to a changing environment, and this helps us to develop a broader perspective and to be more flexible in our interpretation of the past as well as our expectations for the future.

Compassion is a generous, empathic love for all living things. Compassion includes acceptance, appreciation, and forgiveness but also proactively creates connections that inspire trust and promote well-being. When we glow with the warmth of compassion, we promote an optimistic environment where we and other people can feel valued. We can compassionately listen to our hearts, the words of other people, and the breezes that rush through the trees to discover and understand what is happening within and around us, rather than impose our incomplete and unclear insecurities, anger, and judgments which suffocate opportunities for learning and transformation.

I have learned to see the world through my own unique eyes, unspoiled by other people's expectations and disappointments. At the same time, I have learned to continually expand that vision based on what I learn through different and more challenging life experiences. By keeping an open mind and heart, trusting ourselves and the process of life, and honoring the distinct contribution that each person is capable of making, we can compassionately and peacefully interact with others. We can give and receive with ease, sharing with others out of joy rather than a sense of duty or obligation.

Some of my decisions and actions have been driven by guilt rather than by gratitude. As a child, I observed and experienced a great deal of suffering and injustice and did not try to stop it. Even though I was a helpless and vulnerable child, the guilt I felt led me to a life of activism where I have done what I can to protect others by influencing policies and programs. While my guilty conscience resulted in a wonderful and fulfilling vocation, my past can only take me so far into the future. To continue to be motivated and effective in my work, I recognize what happened in the past and its role in my life while basing my current actions on more comprehensive values, rooted in gratitude. I am grateful for all of my life experiences and what they have taught me. They have made me who I am today — a generous and compassionate person.

Over time, the meaning of those experiences has changed. I have wasted so much of my life — my energy and my time — ruminating over things that happened long ago. In many cases, I can no longer remember exactly what happened or why; I can only tap into the anger, guilt, shame, and other feelings that resulted from those experiences. These feelings are provoked by difficult interactions with others or by current events in which there is a great deal of conflict. In the past, I approached much of my life as a problem that I needed to fix or as a series of chores to be completed. I now realize that my life has been a process of learning to be with myself and to interact with others in a way that reflects my true and total self, and that criticism of myself and others alone does not result in sustainable change or happiness. Every moment I hold onto anger is another moment that is wasted.

Compassion resonates deeply with my values, but it also has an impact when expressed internally and externally. When I can, I choose to be compassionate, rather than critical, as my contribution to the well-being of humanity. It also makes me feel better about myself!

Chapter Ten
Perception Re-conception #8:
From Full to Empty

Imagine that within your mind there is a master control center. This center has all kinds of flashy buttons and knobs as well as gauges to indicate our stores of various types of fuel. We have similar systems in our automobiles. Gauges tell us how much gasoline and oil are in their respective tanks and how much air is in each of our tires. Our vehicles have a finite capacity for these and other supplies; our cars have, for example, a gas tank and if we fill up beyond that point the gas would spill all over (causing a fire hazard!).

As we drive along the road, or meander the roads of our lives, we regularly check our gauges to make sure we have adequate supplies to complete our journey. If the gauges in our car indicate that something is getting low, we can stop at a gas station to restore our supplies. If our internal gauges tell us that our energy is being depleted, refilling is not quite so simple. We each have our own way of filling up, of restoring our energy. And we all travel different paths that put unique strains on our energy supply.

Unlike cars and other machines, human beings have more sensitive and complex systems that have the ability to use multiple resources as emotional, intellectual, physical, and spiritual fuel. Our systems are also differentiated by their inverted nature. To keep a car running efficiently, we need to keep all of our supplies as full as possible. Full is the default setting for a machine, and the regular reset point. For a person to run efficiently, and with profoundly meaningful purpose, we must base our fuel choices on a reset point of empty instead.

When our default setting is full, we gorge ourselves on whatever we can get our grubby little hands on to maintain feelings of satiety. Our feelings of fullness become normalized, and we ache when emptiness encroaches. We become greedy, and hoard both tangible and intangible things. We fill our lives with material objects, toxic emotions, superficial friendships, unhealthy food, excessive work, drugs, and other unnecessary, even harmful items that create the illusion of fullness. While it seems as though they may be energizing us in the short term, over time these things will deplete our energy and convert what is left into a very hungry monster that can never get enough. We become addicted, and the more we feast the more fuel we need.

To keep ourselves full, we cling as tightly as we can to whatever we can. If we start to loosen our grip or let go, that hungry little monster starts to gnaw its way through our minds and hearts. It tells us that if we let go, we will need to expend our limited energy to find something else as a replacement. That something else may be undefined or out of reach, and thus it is easier to keep holding on to what we already have whether or not it adds value or beauty to our lives. We cling to a lot of things in our lives, including possessions, relationships, our identity, ideas, and memories, due to fear of emptiness and because substitutes are not readily at our disposal.

I live in a neighborhood that has an informal sharing system. If we put items of relative value out at the curb early enough on a garbage day, they will surely find a new home within a few hours. I recently decided to put six dinner table chairs out at the curb. I purchased them nearly nine years ago, along with my house, but they no longer reflected the type of possession that I desired in my home. I was not sure if I would replace the chairs, or if I would need the space that their absence created, but I knew that indefinitely keeping them in that same place would continue to sap my energy every time I saw them or sat down in them.

About two hours after I put the chairs outside, I heard an idling truck and two women talking near my front door. I went outside to speak with them. They were extremely grateful for the chairs, and shared abundant gratitude and blessings. I told them to come back in a week or two for the table, which, I advised them, did not match the chairs but that difference could be disguised by a tablecloth.

I felt a huge sense of relief when I walked back into the house. Those chairs, which I no longer loved, were gone from my life forever. I would no longer need to look at them every day. I would never sit on them again. Despite the memories that I have made with friends and family sitting on those chairs and sharing meals and good times together, I did not at all regret letting them go. I gave away something that no longer added value to my life while simultaneously making a neighbor very happy and creating more openness in my home and life.

We cling to our possessions for a lot of reasons. They were a gift from a beloved relative or friend. They are associated with memories. We don't know how we would replace them. We might need to use them someday. Someone we know might need to use them someday. But when our possessions sap more energy than they produce, letting them go can help us to feel more free and happy. When we are motivated to reverse our low self-esteem, we may fill up with more and more things to build something of special significance up in our lives. At some point, we need to say, "I am enough, more than enough" and trust the process of life.

Relationships are another area in which many of us cling. We work hard to maintain or improve unhealthy or destructive relationships because we are afraid of being alone. We attach ourselves to other people and their ideas or accomplishments rather than building up our own competencies. Sometimes, out of fear of despairing loneliness, we change our appearance or beliefs in order to be closer to other people or groups of people.

While some people have a fluid identity, and lose themselves by changing to fit with the situation or desired social groups, others cling desperately to their identity and refuse to modify their self-conception in response to a changing environment and new life experiences. Components of our identity may remain static, such as our cultural background or birth order, but our interpretation of the meaning of these aspects of ourselves may evolve over time. Other parts of our identity, particularly those that are temporary by design or are superficial, may serve as a crutch to bolster our self-esteem. After I left a six-year stint as an executive director, it was difficult to let go of this title and status. It was how I identified myself for a long time, and how I was known to others in my community. Because I worked many long hours and enjoyed my work, it was very predominant in my identity composite. When I left this job, there was a huge gap in my identity and it was very uncomfortable for a few years. I had to rewrite the script for my self-description, making it more inclusive and dynamic.

People also cling to ideas. Our ideas are part of our identity and provide us with a framework to make sense of the world. When conflicting information challenges our ideas, it can be difficult to listen and understand the other side. Yet, when we cling to our ideas, it is impossible for us to learn. We need to make room for new information. The most important part of learning is letting go of what we already know — loosening up our grip on ideas and beliefs that we take for granted as the complete and unwavering truth.

We also cling to our memories. The past is often romanticized or demonized as we recall what we have experienced. When we experience trauma, it can be difficult to build a new life because we can never be exactly who we were before; yet, we long for the safety and simplicity of that former life. We can be stuck in the past, and refuse to accept or appreciate current trends or modern advances. If we simply enjoy wearing orange polyester bellbottoms, there is probably no harm done. If we show up to work every day at a factory that closed down and left our town 20 years ago, then our ability to live a full life now is hindered. When we let go of those memories that are holding us back, and the hold they have on our lives, we become free to live in the moment, explore opportunities, and make intentional choices to create a purposeful life in the present.

In addition to clinging to things, ideas, and people, we sometimes also measure the value of our lives in absurd ways. The more income we have, the better (or so we too often think), and because there is no limit we can never be full if we choose to pursue this as a goal. Some people collect social media friends, likes, and shares as status symbols. Other people collect sports cars or coins or spoons from tourist attractions. There is nothing wrong with earning money or collecting even silly, useless objects; but when their pursuit creates an obsession that overshadows other areas of our life and detracts from our well-being, we need to shift our focus from full to empty. Our goal becomes not to have everything, but to have special things that are valuable to us.

There is a pervasive insatiation that drives many people, myself not necessarily excluded. No matter how much we have, we always want more or something else. We have unyielding ambition, collect achievement after achievement, and acquire things to project our carefully constructed identity. That's all good when things are going well, but no matter who we are, and how fortunate and brilliant and amazing and special and perfect we are, we will eventually feel a tremendous sense of failure. And if we are, again myself not necessarily excluded, the type of person who can never seem to achieve our greatest ambitions — and we rely on this as a measure of success in our lives — then we will never truly be happy. We will be plagued with a chronic dissatisfaction and yearning that overwhelms us and provokes us to make choices that don't fully align with our values, leading to poor consequences in our lives as well as the lives of other people.

Feeling full gets in the way of feeling fulfilled. When our minds and our environment are filled up, with no room to move or grow, it is difficult to see clearly and to maneuver. We constrict ourselves slowly over time until it reaches the point that there is no space for other options. We lose our ability to choose, regardless of our desire for free will or to pursue a new direction in our lives. It is the exploration and pursuit of ideas and things, the life journey, that provokes our sense of wonder and makes us question our purpose. As we start accumulating, clinging, and filling up, if we feel that we have "made it" and reached the full point by achieving everything we desire, we lose out on opportunities to have new life experiences and to learn from those experiences. Conversely, if we feel that we can never possibly make it because we do not have the ability to reach that fictitious point, then we will not fully engage in the process of our lives.

The feeling of emptiness can be terrifying, but it can also be liberating. We can think of emptiness has having a clear and calming presence, and a heart full of perfect peace. The way we interpret the concept of emptiness has real consequences in our lives. It influences the way we feel about ourselves and the choices we make. If we think that emptiness is nothing, and nothing is bad and to be avoided at all costs, then we will create a disposable junky life by arbitrarily filling ourselves up with things we don't need, harmful ideas, and people who do not share our values. But we deserve more than that. We can instead welcome spaciousness and continually create opportunities for adventure and possibility.

We can create more space for fulfillment by releasing our excesses. A good way to lighten up is to not take ourselves too seriously. We can release our hold on our self-concept so that it becomes more flexible in relationship to the world around us. Think of a sponge submerged in water. It doesn't change its nature; it is still a sponge and its constitution remains intact. But it softens, and moves in response to objects it encounters. We, too, can be sponge-like in our interactions, letting everything flow through us as we gently caress (emotionally and intellectually, that is) all of the things, people, and ideas that pass our way. We don't need to grab everything we see and hold on to it for potential use at some point in the future.

There are many other excesses that we can release, including mind clutter, toxic thoughts, worry, weight, ugly objects that take up space (like my dining room chairs), emotional baggage, jealousy and envy, destructive relationships, and guilt. All of these things, while perhaps useful at one time, can stand between us and our ability to live a full, free, and happy life.

To promote emptiness, and enjoyment thereof, we can create habits around daily cleansing rituals that purify our minds, bodies, and spirits. These rituals might include housecleaning and de-cluttering, taking a luscious bubble bath, burning incense or sage, eating clean, green foods, sweating through sustained physical movement, crying to release emotions, and meditation to quiet our minds and find still spaces in our hearts. All of these practices can be easily done for little to no cost and they remind us of the loveliness of emptiness so that we no longer feel the need to grasp and cling.

As a teacher, my goal is to open my students up to possibilities rather than fill them up with knowledge. Yes, I know a lot because I have a great deal of experience in my field; yet, I don't know everything and I question whether the way things are done and the theories that have been developed about this work are exhaustive and can remain static when people and everything in the world continue to rapidly change. I'm happy to share what I know, but if I can help my students to discover something new on their own, then I truly feel like I have achieved progress as an educator. This style of teaching offends many products of our industrial revolution throwback education system as evidenced by the handful of reviews each semester that I am the hardest and most unreasonable teacher who ever walked the planet. Living our lives in this way — opening up and creating space rather than filling up — is also counter-cultural. But it is worth exploring and considering, particularly as a means of experiencing emotional balance and well-being.

Everything we desire and everything we need is already within us. It is given to us at birth, and it is something we should cherish. By letting go of the clutter within and around us and the idea of desiring fullness with loving and caring intentions, we can live a light, airy, and blissfully free life.

Chapter Eleven
Perception Re-conception #9:
From Fragile to Delicate

I am a highly sensitive person. If you so much as look at me the wrong way, I might cry or ruminate about it for days. And if you don't look at me at all, I am equally scarred. I am easily hurt by others, even when their intentions are honorable, and have a difficult time getting past these feelings. Years after an infraction has occurred, I may still be reeling and wondering what is wrong with me (and/or the other party or parties involved) to have caused such a disagreeable situation.

This sensitivity has many positive characteristics. I have a sincere empathy for other sentient beings. I am highly intuitive and can tap into my sixth sense. I have the ability to feel a great depth and breadth of emotion. I have a brilliant imagination that takes me to beautiful, although sometimes scary, places. My sensitivity makes me a better and more resilient person who is keenly interested in and is able to understand the outer world — and adapt to it accordingly.

But on the other hand, that outside world is often harsh in contrast to my soft and subdued countenance. Other people are talkative and animated, while I more often tend to be pensive and lost in my thoughts. I am surrounded by conflict, which I both directly experience and indirectly observe, but inside I am continually rebalancing toward peace and harmony. Much of the world seems to have given in to foolish superficiality, while I long for authentic simplicity and grace. Because of my sensitive and responsive nature, it would be impossible for all of these external factors not to have an impact on the way I feel, think, and act.

Sometimes that response is to feel irritable which is often, so I am told, evidenced by the tone of my voice and the words that I choose. I get frustrated easily when I am misunderstood, when I am unable to understand new information or another person's intentions, and when I am unable to complete what ought to be a simple task. My irritability is also provoked by other people's anger, ignorance, and irritability; while I wish to create a buffer of peace, I am not always able to immediately take this high road. I also get irritable when I feel restrained by other people's arbitrary and meaningless rules. And poor customer service, including but especially being forced to speak to a machine over the phone? Forget about it. Sometimes I just feel irritable for no good reason at all; my thoughts and feelings swirl around in a kaleidoscopic blur that makes me feel dizzy, breathless, and unable to fully function. I shut down. When this happens, I overreact to even the simplest infractions of the balance I so desire; I am easily knocked off of the tightrope I need to carefully walk in order to exit the void.

Being irritable is a form of fragility. Irritability is the manifestation of complex feelings that make us vulnerable to our environment and provoke extreme internal and external reactions. The expression of irritability can range from complete withdrawal to raging, screaming, and causing destruction. The way we choose to transform our irritability into words and actions impacts both the way we feel about ourselves and our environment. For me, irritability isn't always a part of my life; it comes and goes — sometimes quite unexpectedly. Knowing that it can pass or emerge at any time without warning has led me to strengthen and draw upon the constants in my life, such as compassion and optimism, to manage these uncomfortable and frustrating feelings when they are present.

Frailty is another, and quite different, type of fragility. Frailty typically makes us think of people who are elderly or chronically ill. People who are physically frail are weak, unable to move freely, and rely on support to make it through the day. When we think of ourselves as emotionally or mentally fragile, we might presume that we are brittle and easy to break. We might shutter ourselves in to avoid being shattered. To function in our daily lives, we might rely upon the time, intellect, strength, or resources of other people or organizations — even when we have the capacity to do much more for ourselves. Feeling as though we are emotionally frail can lead us to become a martyr, and to complain about the great suffering we constantly endure which nobody else could possibly understand, as a means of securing additional attention and assistance.

Perhaps you have used or seen a porcelain teacup. Porcelain is a very delicate ceramic material that can easily break; it is fragile. While a porcelain teacup is designed to be functional and to be used for the enjoyment of warm, soothing beverages, they are often put on a shelf behind glass to protect them from being broken. Rather than being used, these teacups are put on display so that others can see their external features (which are often quite lovely!).

We sometimes treat ourselves like porcelain teacups. When we feel that we are emotionally fragile, and at risk of being chipped or breaking altogether, we put ourselves away on a shelf. We stop taking action and being useful to others. We may put our external veneer on display to maintain some semblance of connection, but really we are isolated and in retreat.

When a porcelain teacup chips or cracks, it becomes difficult to properly use. Chips along the rim, where they most often occur, are uncomfortable against our soft lips. Cracks in teacups may render them useless as the tea (or coffee or other beverage) slips through onto the saucer as it is poured into the cup. If a cup is dropped and shatters, it is nearly impossible to put the pieces back together. And if it can be reassembled, it will never be the same again.

When we protect ourselves by putting ourselves on a shelf, like we might do with a porcelain teacup, we prevent these chips and cracks from occurring. We minimize the risk of shattering and being unable to put our lives back together again. We might think that emotional hardships cause permanent damage, as physical instability might cause permanent damage to a teacup, and therefore justify our exclusion from full engagement in life as a means of protection.

I was born ambidextrous and was able to use both hands equally well. My mother made me choose a primary hand, and I chose my right hand so I would be the same, at least in this respect, as the rest of my family. For all of these years, I have been almost exclusively using my right hand, despite my innate ability. When I try to use my left hand, while it may be a bit easier for me than others who are right-handed, there is a noticeable difference in my abilities between that and my right hand. Anything that we don't use atrophies over time. If I had continued to use both hands, I would be able to use them equally well today. Like our muscles and dexterity, parts of our mind that are not accessed and used will shrink in their capacity. If we hide away on a shelf so that we do not get hurt, our ability to cope and to live a full, healthy life will be diminished. There may be times that we want to hide, protect ourselves, or take a rejuvenating rest. These actions help us to feel safe and give us time to rebuild our emotional reserves. But if we stay on the shelf for too long, it will be harder and harder to leave.

The way we think about the presence, causes, expressions, longevity, and consequences of irritability, frailty, and other forms of fragility impact our ability to cultivate greater strength and resilience. If we think we are

120

fragile, and that our fragility is debilitating and a threat to our mental and emotional health, we will be tempted to use it as a crutch and an excuse to not live in full alignment with our values and aspirations. We can find the courage to be careful, discerning, and cautious without completely withdrawing or shattering to bits. Thinking about our fragility instead as exquisite sensitivity, intentional openness and vulnerability, and delightful delicacy positions us to more fully protect and enhance our emotional well-being.

By thinking of ourselves as exquisitely sensitive, we uplift what we might have thought of as fragility, or a weakness, in the past so that it instead becomes a precious gift with which we would not want to part. We become better able to tune in and appreciate nuances that others overlook or undervalue; this makes life more interesting and meaningful. Our ability to connect with others, and to sense the interconnectedness of all living things, grows. Life situations that we might have once considered to be overwhelming become intriguing mysteries for us to ponder and actively explore. Thus, our capacity to experience life in the moment, create inner stability, more deeply value all life experiences, and generate solutions to challenges is expanded exponentially.

Vulnerability is another strength that we sometimes think of as a weakness. It can be difficult to stay or be soft in what too often feels like a hard world. Unfortunately, genuine kindness has become countercultural in our society (and is therefore super cool!). It may seem easier to respond to this harshness with more harshness to prevent ourselves from being hurt. But when we do this, we cause more pain and suffering for others as well as for ourselves. When we choose to be open and vulnerable instead, we create opportunities to transform our interactions with people and situations that could be considered 'bad' into profoundly significant moments that are life-invigorating and life-changing. Our ingenuity is an engine for personal and social growth; when we choose the freedom of naiveté over the burden of defining and being defined by our limited perceptions, we gain the potential for infinite possibilities. Our vulnerability, when coupled with courage and a thirst for adventure, may lead us to take risks and leaps of faith that result in new intellectual, emotional, or physical discoveries that add beauty, depth, strength, and resilience to our lives as well as the lives of other people.

By allowing ourselves to be sensitive, vulnerable, and flexible, we can create a thoughtful and insightful life full of goodness and delicate loveliness. When we continually seek the most enchanted meanings of our being, we learn to enjoy, cherish, and share the gentle splendor and beautiful bliss of everyday experiences that too often go unnoticed throughout our lives. This practice helps us to transcend the compoundable limitations of fragility to keep us grounded and focused on the things that matter most in life — our values, faith (if applicable), family, friends, the ever-giving natural world, and the communities to which we belong.

Chapter Twelve
Perception Re-conception #10:
From Depletion to Pollination

I have always had a strong desire to share what I have learned with others. Sharing ideas and information with other people helps to solidify my own understanding of things while creating opportunities for other people to learn and strengthen their skills.

As a child, I developed several systems for teaching other people. One of my best friends was three years younger than me, and by virtue of having less life experience was an open book in many areas that I had already explored. I taught her how to do hair and make-up (although I'm sure I made us both look ridiculous), cook (I recall a certain disaster with fruit juice in every crevice of the kitchen), and play the piano (a comparative success!). Around the same time, I established a school in my bedroom where people could learn to dance (I never had a class in my life) and sing. Since the sign-up sheets were in a very exclusive location, my bedroom door, these classes had very low enrollment despite my most honorable intentions. In fifth grade, I got a group of friends together to publish a newspaper for my Sunday School which included stories, games, and pictures.

As an adult, I continued teaching whenever possible. When I was 25, I started a series of workshops for community-based organizations at an anarchist community center. A year or two later, I started teaching entrepreneurship at a local university's community education program. By my early 30s, I was teaching undergraduate credit classes at my alma matter. I started an online school for activists a few years later. Teaching has always been a part of my life for as long as I can remember, and it has taken many different forms over the years.

In the beginning, I approached teaching from a position of dominance and authority. This reflected my personal experience with the American school system. Some people crave this; they want their minds to be filled rather than opened. Teaching was, for me, a mechanism to assert my intellectual and creative superiority — which in the short term boosted my self-esteem but in the long run left me feeing unfulfilled and lonely.

I now realize that teaching is really a form of connection for me. While connecting with other people in a casual, let's hang out sort of way has never been comfortable for me, the structure of the classroom and/or teacher-student relationship has provided me with a basis for developing nurturing, supportive, reciprocally enriching relationships.

Whether or not you have formally been a teacher, we all have the opportunity to share ourselves — our knowledge, ideas, and wisdom — with other people. These opportunities arise as we fulfill our roles as parents, co-workers (or maybe supervisors), organized activity participants, and members of a community. By sharing what we think, believe, and have learned in the past with others, we provoke interesting discussion and thoughtful reflection as well as the development of humanity's potential.

Too often, we are afraid that sharing what we know will take something away from us. I see this a lot in my work, where organizations refrain from sharing 'proprietary information' that could potentially benefit the community and our most vulnerable neighbors. Everyone wants to have control over a domain of knowledge and practice, to be the superhero who can take credit for making a positive community change.

As a writer, I have sometimes refrained from sharing my ideas prematurely for fear that someone else might plagiarize my material or reframe my writing adequately enough to disguise its original source. Every time I send out a query, I have a momentary flinch of fear that the recipient will pitch my ideas to another, more established writer. Other times, I withhold information — as a writer and otherwise — because I am not certain that it is sufficiently unique or valuable. I would hate to pollute the liter-sphere (literature, that is) with poor writing — or my social-sphere with underdeveloped ideas that could be misinterpreted.

In everyday life, we take similar actions all of the time to protect ourselves from embarrassment or exploitation by withholding information and parts of who we are. We may hesitate to help another person or to improve our corner of the world because it puts our reputation at risk. We might withhold a really good idea for fear that someone else will come along, scoop it up, and make a million (or two or three). We do not freely share certain parts of ourselves because we think we might be seen as weak and vulnerable, resulting in other people potentially taking advantage of us.

This competitive stance positions people against each other — neighbor versus neighbor, friend versus friend. It assumes that there are a select few entitled privileged special people who have access to something that is off limits to all others, when all people, in my opinion, are divinely deserving of certain rights. Being competitive, when we could be cooperative, limits our individual and collective growth. While we may see sharing a part of ourselves as depleting a precious finite resource, doing so actually pollinates the minds and hearts of other people so that we all benefit.

Mental illness may complicate our ability to freely share ourselves. Our fears may be magnified while our

125

abilities are at times diminished. We may have been punished for sharing parts of ourselves that were deemed undesirable in the past. We might feel as though we have so little to give, and that sharing our intellectual or emotional reserves would wipe us out entirely — leaving us with nothing but resentment and an extra five sessions of therapy.

The material world is full of finite resources. There is a limited supply of oil, diamonds, trees, coal, and water. Some of these resources are nonrenewable; when they're gone, they're gone. Others can be replenished, but it may take many years for them to be restored. But in the spiritual and intellectual worlds, love and knowledge are infinite. We have allowed the material world, the one with which our interactions may seem the most anchored because of its tangible nature, to define and limit our interactions in those other domains. We withhold our knowledge and our love because we fear that doing so will deplete our limited resources.

Creativity and generosity are magically multiplicative. The more they are used, the more expansive and strong they become. Knowledge and compassionate love cannot be given away like giving a pendant to a special friend. Like creativity and generosity, they can only be shared and multiplied. When we share them, we retain what we originally had and so much more; in addition, what we have shared reverberates through other people and the planet (and perhaps beyond!) indefinitely.

Sharing my experience, knowledge, and ideas with the world makes me more of who I am, more of who I could be. It does not take anything away from me at all. Sharing does not deplete my emotional, intellectual, or creative reserves. It instead creates opportunities for me and other people to cultivate deeper understanding, compassion, generosity, and curiosity. It enriches my life and makes the world a more interesting, and loving, place to live.

Rather than focusing on the acquisition, accumulation, and transfer of material objects, we should shift our attention to the unlimited riches of what we all deserve — a calm mind, a loving heart, and a peaceful soul. These can be developed by sharing with others as well as by accepting and appreciating the generosity of others.

A good friend of mine once told me, in a kind but direct way, that I am a tit for tat person. What he meant by that remark is that I, like most people to some extent, expect equal exchanges in my relationships. When I do something for someone, I expect something equivalent in return. And when I am hurt by someone else, I secretly hope that person experiences a similar level of pain (whether or not it is inflicted by me). It is natural for us to view our relationships in this way; this is what we are taught both directly and through observation. But when we try to control and manipulate other people in alignment with our expectations rather than share and love as generously as possible, we do in fact deplete the reserves in our collective hearts rather than pollinate our hopes for humanity based on our most inspired imaginations. Being aware of these tendencies can help us to make better, more fulfilling choices about our interactions with other people.

We can transcend this limitation on the way we perceive and interact with the world by developing a healing heart. The goal is not to have a heart that is healed (a noun), but rather a heart that is healing (verb). As long as part of the world hurts, so do we. When we hurt, so does the rest of the world. The healing heart continually balances pain and generates love both within ourselves and in the world. The more love we allow ourselves to feel and to share, the more love we can all experience. When we awaken our own hearts, those of our friends and neighbors around us are awakened as well.

This awakening may not be straightforward. We can't expect immediate returns on our generosity. In fact, we can't expect any return at all. Despite what we may believe, the world does not work in a tit for tat way. We do not have the ability to control other people and their responses or reactions to what we do and say. But we also can't allow the limitations of other people to influence our capacity to love. We must not give up on them, when they have so obviously given up on their own capacity to feel and generously share loving thoughts and actions. Our dedication to generosity, to sharing ourselves and our wisdom with no expectation for immediately observable external changes, will plant and pollinate seeds of possibility that expand far beyond our imagination.

You may have experienced a similar phenomenon in your own life. Perhaps you have a personal interest, hobby, or passion. It is something to which you have dedicated many hours of study and practice. Despite your efforts, you do not see improvements. You struggle to perform. And then one day, you reach a tipping point. You enter a natural state of flow that reflects your courageous commitment to something that did not seem possible. It is like a faucet that slowly drips and drips until one day the sink starts to overflow. The spillage waters seeds that had been planted throughout your life, and you start to grow and blossom. It can and does happen. With patience and persistence, we reach a tipping point where we are overflowing with creative and compassionate energy. When we generously share with others, our hearts will overflow with pure, peaceful bliss. Eventually.

Chapter Thirteen
Perception Re-conception #11:
From Dreaming to Being

As an introverted intuitive, I have a very rich inner world. It is there that I spend endless luscious moments playing with possibilities. In my mind, I can freely explore my values, feelings, and ideas without judgment and attachment. At any given moment, I can embark on an exciting quest to discover meaning and purpose regardless of my life circumstances and resources.

My imagination is a paradise. It is an infinite space of beauty. Moments spent in quiet reflection and in creative construction of ideas or potential projects are nurturing and restorative. My mind provides me with a safe place to retreat when I feel overwhelmed by the difficulties of daily life.

But my mind can also be a murky swamp of fear, worry, sadness, anger, and projection. I am not always able to control what enters and exits my mind, nor can I control the timing of these thoughts and feelings. The creative process of allowing ideas to naturally emerge and evolve in my mind, and of exploring multiple ways to understand, use, or transform them, can be an exciting challenge. But I sometimes find it difficult to see beyond this alluring labyrinth of self-exploration. I get trapped in my inner world, and can feel unintentionally oblivious about everything that is happening around me.

After experiencing a great life trauma at a fairly young age, my life was disrupted and put on hold without my consent. I was no longer able to relate and function in the world, one that had previously rejected me and told me I was not mentally well and not good enough because my ideas and means of self-expression deviated from what was expected of a young woman (note the gendered bias that compounded my difficulties). I retreated inward to both make sense of what had happened to me and to protect myself from further judgment and shaming. The world in general became the antagonist in my life story; I felt isolated and as though I would never be able to interact with other people or with my environment in a constructive way.

Later in life, I experienced homelessness. Not the sleeping on the street stereotyped homelessness that most people think of, but the hidden, silent kind that too many young adults experience. I also moved around quite a bit during this time in my life. Inside, I was feeling unsettled and restless. Not only did I feel as though I lacked a safe, stable home from which to base my life, I did not have sufficient orientation to successfully navigate its challenges. My outer world, and the circumstances of my life, were a reflection of what was going on inside of me.

These and other situations forced me to find a safe, trusting, beautiful place within to which I could return at any time when the outer world pulls me away from this center. I have learned to create a strong sense of place in my heart, and to feel at home in my body and in the world. Regardless of my location or life circumstances, I can always feel the sense of sanctuary that comes along with having a home worthy of my investment. That home is within, and it travels along with me wherever I go.

I have been a homeowner, that is, the owner of a physical structure, for nearly a decade. Despite my love for my home, and the lovely aforementioned bat-friendly urban environment lush with trees and flowing water in which it is situated, there are parts of it that cause me a lot of stress. It requires constant upkeep, more so than a newer or fully rehabilitated home would likely require. In addition to ongoing maintenance related to the flooring, foundation, roofs, and other components of the home, my house's living space also requires continual attention. No matter how much I clean and organize, keeping my house tidy is a never-ending project.

Because my attic is the least often used area of my house, it has become a space that collects objects that are not of any immediate use. And because I have this huge space available, I have been collecting and storing objects that belong to relatives as well. Over the years, as my attic has become more full, it has also become cluttered and disorganized. This space, which I once envisioned as a working art studio and hangout space, has deteriorated to the point that it no longer reflects a purpose aligned with my values.

My attic is a bit like my brain. It accumulates useless thoughts and ideas that take up precious space. Like my attic, my mind is in need of tender loving care to restore it to its original pristine state so that it can serve as a resource to help me pursue and fulfill my life vision. It needs to be decluttered, and I need to develop a filtering system so that further unnecessary accumulation does not take place.

Our minds and the world in which we live are intricately interconnected. The world reflects to us what we project in our minds. And our minds reinforce what we see in the outer world. We do not need to choose or prioritize our inner or outer worlds, or to position them against each other in any way because they are interactive. What inside of us has an external impact and vice versa.

This is not to say that we are fully in control of, or responsible for, the entirety of our life circumstances. There are many other people and things that influence our opportunities and choices. Our environment is not fully a reflection of our values, or of our value as a human being. The world responds to us, and us to it, but there is not a direct correlation between what we think and what we experience. We can't just invest our time in thinking about the kind of world we want to live in, and then expect that it will magically appear. We need to take action.

I can be a terrible procrastinator. It can be difficult for me to start projects, and when I do, they often remain incomplete — sometimes for years. I could fill an entire book with descriptions of the many projects that are currently ongoing in my life. I sometimes forget that I started something, and years later I will find a notebook or computer file that reminds me of a once brilliant idea that never fully came to fruition.

When I procrastinate, I am mentally creating a guarantee or assurance that there will be a tomorrow in which the project can be completed. Future time seems much more plentiful than what is available to me right now, even though it will be filled with the completion of more and more projects and activities. I can look forward to a rich and fulfilling future in which I will have so many interesting things to do. But the postponement of my life in this way is a gamble; tomorrow isn't guaranteed. I am also taking a chance that the future will not reveal opportunities to do and experience things that I am now unable to imagine. Procrastination also robs the present moment of its joy, and withholds from the world amazing ideas and opportunities that might otherwise be experienced by many people.

Yet, my procrastination is typically rooted in nothing but the best of intentions. It usually derives from a desire to share an idea with others that could potentially add something valuable their lives, or to bring order to some area of my life. My procrastination is also based in my diverse and expansive interests; because I see the beauty in so many things, I continually explore many possible projects.

When I put something off until later, I am feeling and internally expressing an intention to do something even though I am not able to (or choose not to) invest my precious time in this endeavor at the present moment. It holds space for something that I just cannot do right now. Procrastination acknowledges the value of something and commits us to doing it for a period of time, sometimes indefinitely.

When our intentions are in alignment with our values and hopes for the future, they will eventually result in some form of activity or change in our lives. This might be a refreshed attitude, the pursuit of a new profession, or taking a cooking class. It could be anything, really. When we sit with our intentions for a long time, like we do when we procrastinate, they might evolve to become something even better. This book is an example of how this can happen. When I first conceptualized *Whole Happy and Healthy*, I thought it was going to be about alternative treatments for mental illness such as acupuncture, aromatherapy, and yoga. But as my intention to write stayed within me over a prolonged time period, those ideas shifted and expanded to what you are now reading. As I started writing, my intentions for this book responded by transforming in accordance with the concepts I developed and their potential to help myself and other people.

My intentions and actions were in communion, and developed in concert. If I had not started to write, my intentions about the content and context of the book would have similarly been stifled. Action is the articulation of our intentions. It is how our intentions are expressed and lead to results. But action also influences our intentions as we test our theories in the real world.

In addition to procrastinating when it comes to bigger projects and possibilities, we can also hesitate to fully engage with everyday life by withdrawing to the safety of familiar ideas, people, and places. This retreat, when based in fear, prevents us from learning and experiencing the enjoyment that typically accompanies exciting new experiences. By focusing on 'why not' rather than 'what if,' we can more fully appreciate and experience the gifts offered by the present moment.

Procrastination, or otherwise failing to take action despite our desires, is typically the result of being over-attached to the past or to the future. Disappointments may cause us to feel stuck and unable to move forward. Being filled with a sense of anticipatory joy for what might happen in the future may bring more meaning to what seems like an otherwise dull and dreary life. Rather than searching for something that has been lost, or waiting for something to occur which may never happen, we can choose to create and experience something valuable right now. That experience does not need to be to lavish or time consuming to be extraordinary; just taking small steps in the direction of our dreams feeds our sense of purpose and makes the realization of those visions more possible. Small steps add up, over time, to progress and fulfillment.

Our dreams give us hope. They often lead to the discovery of possibilities for our lives and the world in which we live. Dreams make us feel good and as though we can accomplish anything we desire. But without action, we simply can't and won't move forward. At some point, we need to transform from an analyst to a catalyst to create positive change in our lives. Incessant rumination can prevent us from integrating our inner and outer worlds through action.

We can become more balanced by seeing our inner world and all that surrounds us as interconnected and part of greater whole. Everything we do, every thought, every dream, has meaning and an impact. We can choose to consistently feel and act in accordance with our highest values and most vibrant vision, gently revealing our inner mysteries through every word and movement. At any given moment, we have the opportunity to fully integrate our mind, body, and spirit so that we are able to discover and realize our goals. We become our dreams, moment to moment, step by step.

Chapter Fourteen
Perception Re-conception #12:
From Life is Strife to Life is Love

Struggle is often viewed as heroic in our society. Struggling means that we have a strong conscience and are able to recognize when something isn't right, we choose to take action when the odds are against us, and we are willing to work hard to realize a better outcome that benefits not only ourselves but potentially other people as well. Struggle is a form of brave and noble engagement with life, and one which is sometimes thrust upon us against our will. It usually builds character and leads to increased awareness, if not an improved quality of life.

Throughout my life, by multiple people and in both implicit and explicit ways, I have been taught that struggle is to be commended. The harder we work, the greater the reward — or so we are told. Hard work and self-sacrifice, regardless of the reward, reflect virtue. Life is all about challenge and conflict. Difficulties are opportunities for growth. These and similar narratives have influenced my perception of my life and the world.

I don't necessarily disagree with any of this. I work hard because I enjoy doing so; it brings meaning to my life and is a strong part of my value system. Life is inherently difficult, and there is a unique, mysterious beauty that emerges when we overcome challenges. But there is a limit to how much we can expend without replenishing our reserves. We can't give of and suppress ourselves endlessly without also gracefully opening up and receiving.

I have found that struggle only goes so far, and that it is often counterproductive to achieving my goal of inner peace. Too much of my life has been a fight — with myself, with other people, and with the world. I have been the worst antagonist possible in my own life so as not to be outdone by someone else who could potentially cause me emotional harm. Society has numerous negative expectations of people with mental illness and we too often adopt those views as our own. Feeling as though I was constantly on the defensive, I have navigated my life as if my identity, ideals, and vision were under constant attack. As a result, I have felt isolated and as though the only way I could understand or break through this social barrier was with some form of metaphorical violence. I mostly achieved this by internalizing my feelings of difference informed by others' voiced negative perceptions of me, perpetuating the cycle of internal and external struggle.

I existed from crisis to crisis for much of my life. Crisis became normal to me. The absence of crisis felt like something was missing. I have created unnecessary challenges and drama to fill this void and I still find myself doing this at times. When everything seems like it is going well, I sabotage myself by making a bad decision or doing something I later regret. While this may be influenced by the impulsivity that is germane to bipolar disorder, this behavior reflects a deeper and more sustained need for balance in my life. It is an attempt to restore myself and my life to a state which feels comfortable. Unfortunately for me, and for many, many people, this 'comfortable' state is actually filled with pain and suffering.

Suffering is something that we all experience. To be alive is to suffer. How can we look around us, seeing a world in turmoil, and not feel an overwhelming empathic ache? How can we live with mental illness and not be devastated by the social and emotional pain of this experience? Suffering develops our emotional repertoire and helps us to feel more deeply connected to other people and the planet. I can't imagine living a full life without also experiencing a great deal of suffering.

But there is a difference between deeply experiencing and feeling the suffering we encounter in our lives and becoming a martyr. Suffering serves a beautiful purpose in our lives when it leads to awareness, understanding, compassion, and healing. But when it leads to self-victimization, resentment, disrupting the harmony of relationships or nature, and the propagation of unnecessary suffering, then our attachment to suffering has morphed it into a distortion of its original form and one that can be very destructive.

Similarly, there is a difference between experiencing negative emotions and having a negative attitude. While emotions come and go, attitudes are deeply engrained into everything we think, feel, and do. Unlike negative emotions, which hold tremendous transformative potential, a negative attitude keeps us stuck in a place where everything in our life seems to be clouded by a pessimistic outlook. It impacts our self-esteem, relationships, and ability to take action.

If we view life as a heroic struggle, or as a place where overcoming challenges is virtuous, or as a process of experiencing deep suffering, we must do so from a grounded place of love. Without this basis, our attitude about life will be marred by an incessant striving for something else, something more, something that fills all of the little holes in our hearts. And too often we will settle for less than we deserve when we seek that something based on an unrecognized need for love.

Striving can also be a virtuous endeavor. Continually seeking to improve or perfect some aspect of our lives can make us a better person or improve the quality of our life experiences. It can lead to the cure for a disease, increased energy efficiency, a breathtaking (and oxygen generating) garden space, or other virtuous outcomes. But when striving becomes a way of life, it can be impossible to simply appreciate the many gifts that surround us. When we strive, our focus can get stuck on things that are not the way we want them to be rather than exploring and appreciating those things that are just as they should be.

I have spent a lot of precious energy in my life looking for ideas and situations to critique and deconstruct. I constantly evaluate and judge everything I encounter from fashion to people to architecture to political perspectives. There is a certain victorious rush I feel when I can find some area to be improved so that it better aligns with my ideals and, I sometimes imagine, the needs of greater society. While being judgmental in this way may feel as if I have successfully gained an edge, it is only because I have positioned myself in conflict with others and privileged my ideals over theirs. And in the long run, this makes me feel disconnected and just plain icky.

When our actions are based on an attitude of conflict and dominance (or submission), we will always find something else to serve as the basis for a fight. Encountering things that are unknown to us or that seem incongruent with our values will typically lead us to attempt to contain or change them rather than understand them, love them, and set them free. We are also frequently at war with ourselves, questioning and contesting our abilities and our value. We are continually enmeshed in ongoing internal and external struggles and for those of us who experience mental illness these struggles can be confusing, overwhelming, and sometimes debilitating.

Yet, when there is no struggle in our lives, it is usually because we have become complacent; we have given up. Struggle provides evidence that we care and that we have the courage to pursue the desires and dreams revealed to us in our hearts and our minds.

Surrender offers a balance between the vacuum of complacency and the agony of struggle. Surrender is not necessarily giving in or giving up; it is accepting that our lives are intended to be an incomplete and arduous journey. It means that we listen carefully to the messages of love reverberating all around and within us. Surrender allows us the space and freedom to explore opportunities without attaching ourselves to the outcome. It is a process based in trust and hope rather than avarice, greed, and competition.

What we truly desire can become clearer to us when we stop trying too hard. When we force ourselves to engage in struggle, we can easily get off track pursuing a meaningless goal or doing so in a way that undermines our values. Sometimes we find ourselves putting all of our energy into pursuing something — such as a job or relationship — only to later realize that it is not what we really want. Stepping back and surrendering to what is, and what could be, creates space for possibilities that we might otherwise overlook. Unlike complacency, when we completely shut down and detach ourselves from our desires, surrender requires us to deeply connect with those desires and to fully engage with life during each and every moment to explore and appreciate the beauty that is within and before us.

Our intentions and the way we do things matter just as much as what we actually do. If we have an honorable goal, but pursue that goal in a corrupt or deceptive way, we are creating conditions where strife — prolonged meaningless struggle — prevails at the expense of love, harmony, and ultimately the achievement of our most precious and dignified goals. Our attitude also influences the degree to which we needlessly struggle. A curious attitude that suspends judgment and nourishes our brains with beautiful, loving thoughts keeps us energized and focused on what matters most as we navigate the stormy waters of life.

Much of our lives is spent doing. We keep ourselves very busy as we strive toward our goals or to distract us from those goals which seem out of reach. We can profoundly influence the quality of our limited time on earth by reducing the amount of time we dedicate to doing, trying, and striving and instead invest those cherished moments into breathing, becoming, and just being. This quiet stillness promotes peace and love in our hearts to calm the tides of our tumultuous dis-eases. Too much of my life has been wasted playing the endless game of avoiding pain and seeking pleasure rather than reveling in the sheer joy of being alive from moment to moment.

I continue to have goals and to work toward those goals. Surrendering doesn't mean that I have given up on myself or on my life. It means that I am OK as I am right now. I am loved and able to love others, and that is all that matters.

I continue to experience struggle, but I keep it in perspective. Since I will one day look at all of the challenges I experience through the lens of a rosier future, I can choose to imbue every moment with an optimistic glow today. Experiencing difficulties also provokes my curiosity and my ability to explore possibilities. The more doors shut in our face, the further we are forced to wander down the hallway of life. This perspective, based on a loving attitude, keeps me from feeling defeated regardless of where my struggles lead me.

Stress is a normal part of life. People like you and me who experience mental illness also experience a lot of stress and simultaneously have a diminished capacity to effectively deal with that stress. Yet, we unintentionally load our lives with unnecessary stress that does not contribute to our well-being when we strive at the expense of self- and other-love. Stress can actually be beneficial when it creatively challenges and invigorates our minds and bodies. In addition to surrendering to what is, which develops our capacity to appreciate and love, we can tap into the benefits of good stress by exploring our intellectual and physical boundaries through new experiences. We can redirect our energy in a way that promotes our health and well-being rather than detracts from it, creating a life lush with loveliness.

Chapter Fifteen
Living the Integrative Model of Emotional Wellness

More than 25 years ago, I was diagnosed with, and treated for, schizotypal personality disorder. I felt like an alien in an unwelcoming world. Today, people often remark about how smart and stylish I am. My intellect and creativity distinguish me from the crowd, yet I (usually) feel like I belong. I have changed quite a bit over the years, but the world has changed even more. The world today is far more accepting of diversity in all areas. But we still have quite a way to go until we fully appreciate and understand differences, including those related to the way our minds function and how we express ourselves.

What kind of a word will we live in, I wonder, in another 25 years? I hope it is a world that values empathy, compassion, and self-determination. A world where all people have the ability and support to pursue and discover deep fulfillment. A world that values holism over fragmentation, and liberation over oppression. A world full of peace. Together, we can help to create such a place.

This book represents my aspirational self. Healing is a process, and one in which I am still deeply immersed. In other words, I do not yet fully live this integrative ideal of emotional wellness at all moments of my life. Not by a long shot. Throughout the three years I took to write this book, I continually referred back to its ideas as a source of both grounding and inspiration. I will reflect upon and integrate these ideas as I go forward in my life, adding additional nuance and depth to their meaning as I become more attuned to the greatness within and all around me and realize my human potential.

Change is the continual convergence of multiple intentions and actions. It occurs when we let go rather than attempt to control and confine. *Whole Happy and Healthy* is intended to be exploratory rather than prescriptive. I hope that it has encouraged you to explore expansiveness and connection rather than the isolating, individualistic, reductionist ideology that too often dominates the approach to understanding and addressing mental illness and emotional difference. This book suggests more than a mindset shift. I hope to encourage an expansion of perceptions and rejection of the notion that it is healthy to confine ourselves to any one particular emotional space. We can create space through our thoughts, actions, and interactions and within this space there are many opportunities for joy, healing, and love.

If you were to travel around the world, you would encounter many different languages. Each of our hearts also has a unique language. Words, ideas, images, sounds, and smells all resonate, or not, with each person in a different way. I imagine that each person who reads this book will take from it something that I did not intend and transform my ideas into something that is meaningful and useful on a personal level. I hope that this book will open up many conversations about mental illness so that together we can develop a more comprehensive and flexible understanding of this phenomenon.

Every moment of our lives is precious and perfect. Happiness is our most natural state of being, and something to which we long to return. Remember that being happy is not a linear, one-dimensional experience. We often think about happiness as if it were a consistently blissful, pain-free state and, as a result, something that is unattainable. Happiness is not an achievement or a reward that yields from sacrifice and hard work. It is a moment-to-moment choice that continually manifests a sense of calming peace and radiant joy. It is the will to experience life as it happens, and to feel connection without attachment. Perhaps happiness is, rather than an outcome, the desire to be open to all of the forms of happiness explored in Chapter Two. Happiness is discovered and cultivated through the interpretation and appreciation of our experiences.

My experiences of mental health treatment have pushed me to fit in and to function. That just isn't good enough for me anymore; I want to flourish. And I want you to flourish, too. While emotional stability is important, emotional resilience can be even more transformative. The ups and downs of my dis-ease have helped me to develop a broad repertoire of ways that I can choose to respond to life's circumstances and changing moods. It is up to each of us to use what we have learned through the experience of mental illness to make the world a more enriching and loving place every day. We can create and fulfill a beautiful and miraculous vision for our lives and our world.

I will close this book with the wish that we will all continue to open our hearts and our minds through compassion, creative exploration, and conversation. Thank you for taking the time to embark on this journey with me. I hope you have discovered ideas, approaches, and new depths to your inner wisdom that will fortify the remainder of your life travels. Be well.

Notes

Notes

Notes

www.ingramcontent.com/pod-product-compliance
Lightning Source LLC
Chambersburg PA
CBHW020521290526
45786CB00002B/700